INTRODUCING THE
MEDIEVAL SWAN

INTRODUCING THE MEDIEVAL SWAN

NATALIE JAYNE GOODISON

UNIVERSITY OF WALES PRESS

2022

www.uwp.co.uk
British Library CIP Data

A catalogue record for this book is available from the British Library
ISBN   978-1-78683-839-1
eISBN   978-1-78683-840-7

Designed and typeset by Chris Bell, cbdesign
Printed by the CPI Antony Rowe, Melksham, United Kingdom

SERIES EDITORS' PREFACE

THE UNIVERSITY OF WALES PRESS series on Medieval Animals explores the historical and cultural impact of animals in this formative period, with the aim of developing new insights, analysing cultural, social and theological tensions and revealing their remarkable resonances with our contemporary world. The series investigates ideas about animals from the fifth century to the sixteenth, and from all over the world. Medieval thought on animals preserved and incorporated a rich classical and mythological inheritance, and some attitudes towards animals that we might consider as having characterized the Middle Ages persisted up to the Enlightenment era – and even to the present day.

We are so grateful to Dr Natalie Goodison for writing this book on the Medieval Swan and permitting us to remember Dr Jayne Wackett in the dedication. Jayne, a wonderful art historian, first proposed this title but sadly died after her proposal was accepted.

CONTENTS

ACKNOWLEDGEMENTS

I AM DEEPLY indebted to many in writing this book. Colleagues, whose scholastic and linguistic expertise is greater than my own have been invaluable, including Dr Corin Corley and Dr Alex Wilson to whom I owe many thanks. The manuscript has been wonderfully improved thanks to the reviewer, the editors, and the preparation team at University of Wales Press. My special thanks to Sarah Lewis, Dr Dafydd Jones, Dr Victoria Blud, and Dr Diane Heath, for their patience and enthusiasm. Many of the photographs in this book were provided through the kindness of organisations dedicated to promoting cultural exchanges of knowledge. These include the British Library, the Bodleian Library, the Bibliothèque nationale de France, Heidelberg Universitätsbibliothek, Frankfurt Cathedral, Washington DC's Library of Congress, Wawel Royal Castle, the Art Institute of Chicago, the Huntington Library, and the National Gallery, London. The commitment of these bodies to intellectual and cultural exchange of knowledge is praiseworthy. Their kindness has made this small book far richer. The remaining costs of photographs for this book were provided through the generosity of Durham University's Department of English Studies and the Vinaver Trust. I am deeply grateful to both organisations for their support. Their generosity has enabled this book to contain colour photographs. Durham University Library was exceptionally accommodating in procuring resources for me in the midst of a pandemic, and I am very grateful to them, particularly to Judith Walton. Durham's Archives and Special Collections librarians were also incredibly helpful in pointing out resources unknown to me: my special thanks to Dr Michael Stansfield. Durham also offered me an Honorary Fellowship to enable me to complete this manuscript. With offices closed and libraries shut during the Covid-19 pandemic, I am thankful to Al Barrat who let me write this book in her home. Writing a book is exacting, the tax even higher in lockdown. In this light, I must offer particular thanks to my husband Francis, who, in the midst of a difficult year, was unwavering to me in his kindness, gentleness, and support. My gratitude to him, I hope, is reflected in this book's dedication.

LIST OF PLATES
AND ILLUSTRATIONS

FIGURES

PLATES

LIST OF
ABBREVIATIONS

Cal. Pat. Rolls (also Cal. Rot. Pat.)	*Calendar of the Patent Rolls*, 1232–1509, Public Record Office, 53 vols (London: 1891–1916)
Close Rolls	*Close Rolls of the Reign of Henry III*: 1247–51, Public Record Office, (London: H. M. Stationery Office, 1922)
DPMA	Durham Priory Manorial Accounts
KHLC	Kent History and Library Centre
OED	Oxford English Dictionary
PCR	Probate Court Records
PG	*Patrologia Graeca*, ed. J. P. Migne, 161 vols (Paris: Garnier, 1857–66)
PL	*Patrologia Latina*, ed. J. P. Migne, 222 vols (Paris: Garnier, 1844–1902)
PRO	Public Record Office
TNA	The National Archives

To the memory of my grandmother,
Jessie Kate Iler Buie,
to the memory of Jayne Wackett,
and for Francis

INTRODUCTION

B EAUTY, ROMANCE, royalty, and death – the swan effortlessly captures human imagination in all its quiet grandeur. Yet questions arise from these innate swan associations: why is the swan so romantic, why is it a regal emblem, why does the Queen own all the swans in Britain – and why is a final performance a swansong?

Answers to these questions about the swan and our emotional connections to this bird lie in the history and culture of medieval Europe. To date, no volume provides a long intellectual history for the medieval swan from 1000 to 1600. Yet it is well-worth doing so. The broad argument of this book is that the swan's identity shifts over time – from a bird known for its death-song to an icon of the European court. The catalyst for this shift, I argue, is the story of the Knight of the Swan, the legendary ancestry of Godfrey of Bouillon, ruler of Jerusalem (1099–1100). Establishing the heritage of the Swan Knight is important precisely because it is not well-known in either British or American culture. However, the stories of the Swan Knight captivated the courts of medieval Europe, influenced medieval culture, and in Germany, shaped topography, literature, and music.

The book explores three main areas: the swan's song, the Swan Knight, and the swan's association with royalty and aristocracy. This book opens by examining medieval views of the swan's natural history. Classical and medieval texts report that the swan's beautiful song heralded its own death (Chapter 1). In medieval literature, the swan is transformative. Often children, and occasionally maidens and angels, turn into swans (Chapter 2). These stories provide the basis for the Knight of the Swan, the mysterious chevalier and alleged grandfather of Godfrey of Bouillon. Conqueror of Jerusalem and one of the nine worthies, Godfrey epitomised the medieval hero, and medieval courts vied to claim Godfrey as their ancestor, elevating the swan to a courtly symbol (Chapter 3). The swan was also a choice dish at medieval banquets, causing the husbandry and ownership of swans to be carefully regulated in England. Swan ownership was identified through swan markings, and over time, the Crown restricted the right to mark swans, defaulting all un-marked swans as property of the monarchy (Chapter 4). The final chapter explores the afterlives of the medieval swan present today.

A Note on the Text
This book provides an academic introduction to the medieval swan. Its scope was not intended to be comprehensive. I have not included all I have found, and I am sure there is more to discover. In a book of few words, I have chosen to prioritise primary source material. The endnotes indicate wider reading. The span of this short book focuses on medieval Europe and regrettably could not incorporate the many fascinating references to the swan in Asia and the Middle East. All photographs have been reproduced with permission or are in the Public Domain.

This book was written during the Covid-19 pandemic of 2020–2. As a result, I have been unable to procure some sources. Greek and Old Irish quotations appear in translation, but the endnotes include a reference to an edition of the texts in their original language. The quotations from Middle English I have translated at my discretion, based on their difficulty. Despite its shortcomings, I hope this book provides a helpful resource for medieval swan scholarship.

European Swans

The swan is thought to be indigenous to Europe. In part this is due to its recorded distribution and migratory patterns, but this is supported by written record and carbon dating. As Mute Swans inhabit Greece and as swans appear in classical medicinal recipes, classical writers were likely familiar with swans.[1] Swan bones have been identified in Roman-Britain burial remains and indicate that the swan existed in Europe to at least the fourth century.[2]

The male swan is a cob, the female a pen, and their offspring cygnets.[3] The swan mates for life, choosing its partner in its third or fourth spring. The pen lays a clutch of five-to-eight eggs and incubates them for thirty-eight days. Each parent contributes to the nest. It prefers to feed on lakes, shores, rivers, and marshland, and its diet ranges from grasses to insects and amphibians. Three types of swans inhabit Europe: Bewick's Swan, the Whooper Swan, and the Mute Swan.

Bewick's Swan (*Cygnus columbianus*) is the smallest of the three (115–27 cm). It inhabits the most northerly regions of the Arctic, and so is nicknamed the 'Tundra Swan'.[4] Its colouring is white, and its bill is yellow with a black tip.

Bewick's Swan has a round head and straight neck. With strong migratory instincts, it breeds in the Palearctic regions of Russia and migrates along the Baltic coastline to winter in Britain, the Netherlands, Denmark, and Germany. It is known for its loud, babbling song. It uses its voice year-round, both in chorus and individually, on water and in flight.

The Whooper Swan (*Cygnus cygnus*) has similar colourings to Bewick's Swan.[5] It too has a straight, long neck and yellow-black bill, but is much larger than Bewick's Swan (145–60 cm). The Whooper breeds in more southerly regions than Bewick's Swan, finding its home in the tundra of Russia, Finland, Iceland and Sweden. It too has strong migratory patterns, wintering along coasts of Britain, Ireland, Norway, and the perimeters of the Baltic and Black seas. It walks well on land and is known for its loud song. The Whooper's strength of sound stems from its unusual anatomy, as it has an extra loop of trachea within its sternum.[6]

The Mute Swan (*Cygnus olor*) is the most well-known swan because it lives in temperate regions and is widely spread across geography.[7] Similar in size to the Whooper, the Mute Swan is distinguished by its graceful, curved neck, its red-orange bill, and its black knob. Its habitation is extensive – ranging from Japan to Egypt, with a concentrated population in Britain. It is partially migratory, meaning only some Mute Swans migrate, particularly those in Iceland. The Mute Swan is known for its relative voicelessness, save for hissing in situations of threat. Its wings, however, make a distinct sound in flight, audible within a one-mile radius. Cygnets are known to sit on the back of the pen. On land the Mute Swan walks awkwardly with waddling motion.

This brief outline reveals that European swans vary in colour, habitation, and song. Intriguingly, some of these characteristics of swans feature in medieval treatises on natural history. The following chapter explores medieval knowledge of swan behaviour, including the prevalent and insistent reference to the swan's song.

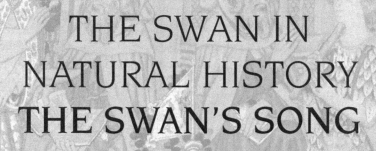

THE SWAN IN
NATURAL HISTORY
THE SWAN'S SONG

C ONTEMPORARY STUDIES of natural history tend to focus on data-driven observations of a creature's interactions within its environment. This contrasts to early medieval studies of natural history, which emphasised a creature's fabulous or unusual qualities. For medieval writers, the swan's most remarkable quality was its beautiful song just before its death. Inherited from classical writings, the swan's song permeated medieval natural history, and from there, influenced medieval art and culture.

ISIDORE OF SEVILLE

The natural world fascinated medieval writers, spurring their academic enquiry. Medieval encyclopaedic works on the natural world frequently included swans. One of the earliest encyclopaedists was Isidore of Seville (c.560–636), who compiled an extensive 'summa' (or summary) of all knowledge in his *Etymologies*. Devoting an entire section to birds, Isidore thought that the swan's name reflected its natural characteristics. He writes:

> Olor avis est quem Graeci κύκνον appellant. Olor autem dictus quod sit totus plumis albus: nullus enim meminit cygnum nigrum; ολον enim Graece totum dicitur. Cygnus

autem a canendo est appellatus, eo quod carminis dulced-
inem modulatis vocibus fundit. Ideo autem suaviter eum
canere, quia collum longum et inflexum habet, et necesse
est eluctantem vocem per longum et flexuosum iter varias
reddere modulationes. Ferunt in Hyperboreis partibus
praecinentibus citharoedis olores plurimos advolare, apte-
que admodum concinere. Olores autem Latinum nomen
est; nam Graece κύκνοι dicuntur. Nautae vero sibi hunc
bonam prognosim facere dicunt, sicut Aemilius ait (4):

> Cygnus in auspiciis semper laetissimus ales:
> hunc optant nautae, quia se non mergit in undas.

The swan is the bird that the Greeks call κύκνος. It is called
'swan' (*olor*) because it is 'entirely' white in its plumage; for
no one mentions a black swan; in Greek 'entire' is called
'ὅλος'. The *cycnus* (i.e. *cygnus*, another word for swan, bor-
rowed, in fact, from the Greek κύκνος just cited) is named
for singing (*canere*) because it pours out a sweetness of
song with its modulated voice. It is thought to sing sweetly
because it has a long curved neck, and a voice forcing
its way by a long and winding path necessarily renders
varied modulations. People say that in the Hyperborean
regions, when musicians are singing to citharas, swans
come flocking in large numbers, and sing with them quite
harmoniously. *Olor* is the Latin name, for in Greek they
are called κύκνος. Sailors say that this bird makes a good
omen for them, just as Aemilius (Macer) says (fr. 4):

> The swan is always the most fortunate bird in omens.
> Sailors prefer this one, because it does not immerse
> itself in the waves.[1]

Isidore links the swan's name to its ability to sing. He derives his precedent of etymologies-as-meaning from the Roman poet Varro (116–27 BC).[2] Isidore appropriates Varro's list to include the swan, making him the first to forge the linguistic connection between 'cygnus' (swan) and 'canere' (to sing).[3] Isidore uses etymologies, not just from Varro, to emphasise the transcendental power of the Word of God. In light of this, it would be natural for the clue to the swan's unique powers of song to be hidden within the swan's very name.

CLASSICAL PRECEDENT

As the most common European swan is relatively voiceless, Isidore's emphasis on the swan's singing ability may come as a surprise. However, the legend of the singing swan and its harmonization to human instruments is recorded by the Roman author Aelian (AD 175–235). He writes that in the Hyperborean regions swans descended upon the Temple of Apollo, sang along with human lyres, and then flew away.[4] Aelian is part of a long line of classical authors who record the swan's song, spanning from Plato to Virgil.[5] Classical writings on swans are extremely important because medieval writers of natural history mined classical sources for swan data, appropriated this information for a medieval audience, and incorporated this data into medieval structures of scientific thought.

One of the most important classical texts on the swan is Plato's *Phaedo* (360 BC). Facing execution, Socrates compares himself to swans which sing joyfully at their approaching death, eager for the world to come in which they will rejoin the god Apollo, whom they serve. Originally written in Greek, the *Phaedo* records Socrates saying:

> And you seem to think I am inferior in prophetic power
> to the swans who sing at other times also, but when they
> feel that they are to die, sing most and best in their joy
> that they are to go to the god whose servants they are
> [...] I believe they have prophetic vision, and because
> they have foreknowledge of the blessings in the other
> world they sing and rejoice on that day more than ever
> before. And I think that I am myself a fellow-servant of the
> swans, and am consecrated to the same god and have
> received from our master a gift of prophecy no whit
> inferior to theirs, and that I go out from life with as little
> sorrow as they.[6]

For Socrates, the swan functioned as an exemplar for facing death. The *Phaedo* highlights two important points about swans: they have prophetic abilities and they sing best before they die. Throughout later literature, these two aspects persistently recur.

Examples of swans singing in death or sorrow are plentiful. Possibly the earliest reference to the swan's death-song is in Aeschylus' (*c*.525–*c*.456 BC) *Agamemnon*. Lying dead beside her lover, Cassandra is described as 'she, who, like a swan, has sung her last lament in death'.[7] In Moschus' 'Lament for Bion' (second century BC) the swan's song personifies grief: 'You swans of Strymon, cry woe beside your waters; with your / lamenting voices sing a dirge such as old age produces from your throats'.[8] Aristotle (384–322 BC) provides one of the first natural histories of the swan in his *Historia Animalium*. He describes the swan's habitat, parenting style, and ability to sing. He states that swans 'are songsters and sing especially at the time of their death'.[9] He even records that sailors have heard swans singing their death-song off the Libyan coast. In *De Oratore*, Cicero (d. 43 BC) describes Crassus' final speech. 'Illa tanquam cycnea fuit divini hominis vox et oratio' (That oration was the swan-song of this inspired genius), writes Cicero.[10] Here the swan's song refers to a final act of greatness before death.

Literary influences also contributed to the classical precedent of the swan's voice. In Ovid's *Metamorphoses* (AD 8), the swan's song illustrates passionate grief. As the nymph Canens searches frantically for her husband, whom Circe has turned into a woodpecker, 'illic cum lacrimis ipso modulata dolore / verba sono tenui maerens fundebat, ut olim / carmina iam moriens canit exequialia cygnus' (there, she poured out her words of grief, tearfully, in faint tones, in harmony with sadness, just as the swan sings once, in dying, its own funeral song).[11] In the *Aeneid* (29–19 BC), Virgil links the swan's song with its long neck: 'Et longa canoros / dant per colla modos' (And from their long throats utter their tuneful strains).[12]

In *Aesop's Fables* (fifth century BC), the swan's song is crucial to its identity. A man keeps a swan for its voice and a goose for the table. The man fetches the goose to eat, but being dark, he catches the swan by mistake. The swan, thinking it is about to die, begins to sing, and is recognised by its voice.[13] This fable offers the idea that swans sing only when they die, hence their last great labour. The swan also became a symbol of the poet. Homer is called the 'Swan of Meander', and Virgil the 'Mantuan Swan'.[14] The swan-as-poet may stem from the bard Orpheus, known for his poetry and song. After his death, his soul was transformed into a swan and his lyre was hung as a constellation in the sky.[15]

However, not all writers believed the swan's song to be true. The prominence of the swan's song in classical texts is certainly incongruous with the only breed of swan that inhabits the Mediterranean – the Mute Swan, known for its lack of song. Pliny (AD first century), for one, challenges the truth of the swan's song, even examining the evidence first-hand: 'Ut arbitror aliquot experimentis' (A false story as I judge on the strength of a certain number of experiences).[16]

Classical information on the swan's song continued to be perpetuated throughout late antiquity. Lactantius (AD *c*.250–*c*.325) thought the swan's song to be inferior to the Phoenix's: 'Sed neque olor moriens imitari posse putetur' (Nay, let not the dying swan be thought capable of imitating it).[17] Heraclius (in AD 426) employed swan metaphors to compare his own inferior preaching abilities to that of his esteemed predecessor, Augustine of Hippo. During his first sermon, Heraclius stated: 'Ciclada clamat, et cygnus tacet' (The cricket chirps, and the swan is silent).[18]

These classical and early Christian authors illuminate Isidore's description of swans. Isidore's writings on swans chime with that of Varro, Aelian, Aemilius Macer, and Virgil. Given this, it is surprising that Isidore does not mention that swans sing best at and prior to their death. When later medieval writers copied Isidore's description of swans, nearly verbatim, ultimately, they rehearsed, and eventually modified, classical perception of swans. Medieval conceptions of swans are steeped in classical precedents.

EARLY NATURAL HISTORY

Isidore influenced early studies on medieval natural history. These early schools viewed the natural world as an exhibition of God's character. Studying the natural world was a means of unlocking hidden aspects of God himself. Proponents of this view were Origen of Alexandria (AD *c*.184–*c*.253) and Augustine of Hippo (AD 354–430). For Origen, 'per haec quod visibilis hic mundus de invisibili doceat et exemplaria quaedam caelestium contineat positio ista terrena' (this visible world may teach about the invisible and that earth may contain certain patterns of things heavenly).[19] The sensory world reflected heavenly archetypes, reinforcing a similitude between the natural world and spiritual. Clark writes that for Augustine 'the ultimate function of all living things, as part of the great cosmos, was to reflect the Creator, to be the mirror by which the invisible God became visible'.[20] The natural world contained spiritual truth. Medieval writers frequently interpreted the natural world through spiritual allegory. The earth was situated in an hierarchy amongst the heavenly cosmos, and the natural world resonated with the power of the spheres, even imbibing their marvellous properties.[21] To the medieval mind, animals could reflect God's character, unlock spiritual truths, and contain marvellous abilities.

Many writers reinterpreted classical and early medieval texts through a spiritual lens. One of the first to add a spiritual allegory to the swan was Rabanus Maurus (789–856), Archbishop of Mainz. Drawing heavily on Isidore's *Etymologies*, Rabanus copies Isidore's description of the swan nearly verbatim in his *De Universo*. He adds only one extra line: 'Cygnus cervicis altae, superbia exprimitur'

(The swan signifies pride, by its long neck).[22] Maurus reconstitutes Isidore's swan and adds spiritual significance to one of its physical attributes.

The moralising bent to natural history, illustrated by Rabanus, became widespread in medieval writings. This likely derived from the *Physiologus*, a third-century Greek text, popular throughout the Middle Ages, that interpreted natural history through spiritual allegory.[23] The *Physiologus* inspired medieval bestiaries.[24] Bestiaries spotlighted creatures, highlighted their fabulous properties, and gave them spiritual significance. This was done, so that, in the words Thomas of Cobham (d. 1327), 'per ipsas creaturas non solum inspiciamus quid nobis utile sit in corpore, sed etiam quid sit utile in anima' (through the same creatures we may contemplate not only what may be useful to us in the body, but also what may be useful in the soul).[25] Although the *Physiologus* did not include swans, bestiaries did, deriving their swan data directly from Isidore. Many twelfth-century bestiaries follow Isidore's account verbatim, emphasising the swan's song, but mentioning neither its death-song nor its spiritual allegory.[26]

However, many later bestiaries did moralise the swan. Hugh of Fouilloy, a twelfth-century Augustinian friar, was influential in promoting the swan's spiritual allegory. His *Aviarium* is a moralising book of birds modelled upon bestiaries.[27] Influenced by Isidore and Rabanus, Hugh expanded the natural history of the swan, including the swan's song at death. For each of the swan's natural characteristics, Hugh adds a moralising line. Hugh begins by describing the swan's colouration: 'Cignus plumam habet niveam, sed carnem nigram' (The swan has snowy plumage, but black flesh).[28] The reference to black flesh seems to refer to the skin of a plucked swan or the colour of its meat when roasted. Less likely, but just possible, is that it may refer to the black feet of the swan, contrasting against its white plumage and unseen when the swan is in water (Figure 1). Hugh states that this contrast between white and black symbolises the hypocrite: the Christian who outwardly appears pure but inwardly hides mortal sin ('quia peccatum carnis simulatione velatur'). The moralisation plays upon the word flesh – the 'carnem' of the swan compares to the 'carnis', of bodily or 'fleshly' appetites of carnal sins. The swan's neck, erect and proud, symbolises

Figure 1: *Bestiary image of swan, thirteenth century. London, British Library, MS Harley 4751, fol. 41v. © British Library Board. The swan appears to be accurately drawn, reflecting colourings of the Mute Swan. The swan symbolised hypocrisy in bestiaries, with its snowy white plumage contrasted against its hidden 'carnem nigram' or dark flesh.*

man's pride in his worldly possessions ('possessione ad tempus gloriatur'). The swan's death-song, both sweet and sad, reflects the proud man's attitude in death – delighting in the world and lamenting his wrongdoings. Most shockingly, the swan's common fate in the Middle Ages – being plucked, spitted and roasted over the fire – is the fate of this wealthy, proud man in Hell. In death he is 'exuitur mundana gloria' (stripped of his worldly glory); he is roasted ('torretur') by the flames of hell; and like the spitted swan, whose fat drips into and fuels the fire's flames, so the wealthy man 'fit cibus ignis' (becomes food for the fire). For Hugh, the swan reflects the dangers of pride and worldly possessions, and he names their deadly consequences if unchecked.

Hugh's *Aviarium* was copied in over 125 manuscripts, many illustrated, and was incorporated into second-family bestiaries, such as Bodleian MS 764.[29] This bestiary copies Hugh's description of the swan nearly verbatim – including his moral interpretations. The Latin translation of MS 764 reads: 'The white-plumaged swan represents successful deception; just as the white feathers hide black flesh, so dissimulation hides a sinful heart'.[30] Perhaps bestiary illuminations of the swan reflect its allegorical significance. Images such as Harley MS 4751 depict a white swan above water, with black feet hidden beneath the waves, which may symbolise hypocrisy by contrasting displayed whiteness against concealed blackness (cover and Figure 1).

Many bestiaries, such as Harley MS 4751 accurately depict the identifying marks of the Mute Swan as described by modern ornithologists: the graceful curve of the neck, the downward tilt of the head, the striking red-orange bill, black knob, and black feet (cover and Figure 1).[31] Morrison notes that bestiary depictions of the swan shifted from the black bill, found in early bestiaries, to an orange bill – likely to reflect the Mute Swan's colouring.[32] This accuracy attests to a familiarity with the swan by both medieval authors and their audiences.

Because bestiaries were enormously popular and widely copied, the swan became known as a symbol of hypocrisy. For example, Jacques de Vitry (1180–1240) includes the swan in his list of sermon illustrations. The swan's white plumes and black flesh, he explains, signifies the one who appears pious but is without virtue ('qui speciem pietatis habentes, uirtutem eius abnegant').[33] The swan-as-hypocrite was so widespread it was even employed by Chaucer. He describes the friar as 'fat as a whale, and walkynge as a swan, / Al vinolent as botel in the spence' (fat as a whale and walking like a swan, / As full of wine as a bottle in the wine-cellar).[34] Medieval friars were mendicants, known for their vows of poverty and chastity. Comparing the friar's gait to the Mute Swan's well-known waddle epitomises hypocrisy: a fat, drunken friar has obviously abandoned his vows of poverty and abstinence.[35] The swan-as-hypocrite appears on the Grail Quest – a world in which knights struggle to discern spiritual realities from earthly ones. Sir Bors has a dream of a white swan and a black bird and must choose which to follow. The swan offers Bors riches and beauty, while the black bird, cryptically, instructs Bors not to despise its black hue.[36] A demon disguised as a hermit interprets this dream for Bors. The demon tells Bors the swan represents a beautiful paramour whose love he should accept. However, this interpretation is merely a ruse to tempt the knight to fornicate in the Castle of Maidens. Bors is later told:

> Li cisnes est blans par defors et noirs par dedenz, ce est li ypocrites, qui est jaunes et pales, et semble bien, a ce qui defors en apert, que ce soit des serjanz Jhesucrist; mes il est par dedenz si noirs et si horribles d'ordures et de pechiez qu'il engigne trop malement le monde.

> The swan is white without and black within, it is the hypocrite, who is fair-hued and pale and who gives every outward sign of being among the servants of Jesus Christ: but inwardly he is so black and hideous with the sludge of sin that he deceives the world most grossly.[37]

The swan was a spiritual metaphor to warn Bors not to be deceived by outward appearances.

Perhaps because it was a symbol of hypocrisy, the swan rarely represented Christ in medieval art. This was a function primarily reserved for the pelican. Thought to pierce its own breast to both revive and nourish its young, the pelican functioned as Christ symbol, frequently depicted in illuminations surrounding the crucifixion.[38] However, the swan's spiritual symbolism could be positive. For example, a thirteenth-century French prose bestiary likens the swan's death-song to the Christian soul, joyful in adversity: 'Cest chine que si bien cante encontre sa mort, senefie l'ame qui a joie en tribulation' (This swan which sings so well against its death signifies the soul which has joy in tribulation).[39] Evoking the *Phaedo*'s interpretation of the swan's dying song as a joyful strain, this bestiary interpretation is drawn from Scripture, invoking believers to count suffering as joy (James 1:2). A similar sentiment is echoed in the *Tretyse of Loue* (*c*.1493), where the swan's death-song 'signefyeth the soule that hathe loye in try-bulacion' (signifies the soul that has joy in tribulation).[40] Alexander Neckam (1157–1217) considers the swan's transformation from ash-grey cygnet to downy white adult. He takes this transformation to symbolise Christian conversion and/or sanctification:

> Quid quod cygnus in aetate tenella fusco colore vestitus esse videtur qui postmodum in intentissimum candorem mutatur? Sic sic nonnulli caligine peccatorum prius obfuscari, postea candoris innocentiae veste spirituali decorantur.

> What shall we say of the swan who seems to be clad in its tender age in a dusky hue but before long changes to a dazzling whiteness? Even thus some men seem first to be darkened by a cloud of sin, and afterwards are clad in the spiritual raiment of the dazzling whiteness of innocence.[41]

Here the swan symbolises the repentant sinner as well as the believer's steady progress toward holiness. Aspects of the swan's physical features became fodder for spiritual interpretation. The swan was frequently a symbol of hypocrisy, but occasionally described the Christian's earthly experiences.

ARISTOTELIAN NATURAL HISTORY

In the twelfth-century a newly-discovered model of natural history arrived and sought, through empirical science, to discover the rational structure of the natural world.[42] Medieval natural history began to shift away from moralisation and towards the observation of organisms in their natural habitats. Kellie Robertson describes medieval debates between the two camps: the 'Augustinian model' – that 'nature was a veiled expression of divine will and therefore impervious to the gaze of the natural philosopher'; and the 'Aristotelian model' – as 'nature's regularity manifested an ethical system that could lead the sensitive observer to moral truths'.[43] The Aristotelian model of natural history derived data from close observation through first, second, or perhaps third-hand experience.

Aristotelian observation of swans appears in the work of Bartholomaeus Anglicus, a thirteenth-century English Franciscan (d. 1272). In his *De proprietatibus rerum*, Bartholomaeus expounds upon Isidore's description of swans, with information likely derived from observation – such as the swan's distinctive mating dance. The English translation of Bartholomew's text (1397) reads:

> Whanne þe swan is in loue he secheþ þe female and plesiþ hire wiþ byclippinge of þe necke and drawiþ hire to hymward and ioy[neþ] his necke to þe females necke as it were byndynge þe neckes togidr.

> When the swan is in love he seeketh the female and pleaseth her with beclippings of the neck and drawith her to himward and joineth his neck to the female's neck as it were binding the necks together.[44]

Well-recorded by ornithologists, this mating dance is known as the 'precopulatory display', which involves head-dipping, synchronous actions, and entwined necks.[45] Another user of

Aristotelian methods is Thomas of Cantimpré (d. 1272) who analyses swan migration.[46]

One of the greatest Aristotelian scholars of the Middle Ages was Albertus Magnus (Albert the Great) (c.1200–80), Bishop of Regensburg. His magisterial zoology *De animalibus* provides one of the most extensive taxonomies of natural history. A detailed commentary on Aristotle's *De animalibus*, Albertus' tome incorporates a catalogue of species inspired by his student Thomas of Cantimpré, adding personal comments, many deriving from observation.

Albertus was deeply interested in how the swan exists and interacts in its environment. His description of swans is wonderfully accurate. He places the swan in the goose genus 'anseris', where the swan sits today among the subfamily 'anserinae',[47] He notes that the swan feeds on grasses, vermin, eggs of fish, and seeds from crops – all of which is true.[48] Its feeding habits, he writes, are enabled by a serrated bill, which strains mud to find food, which it then chews. This too is accurate. He describes its colouration, mating habits, means of generation, nesting character- istics, and parenting methods. He continues, 'Haec avis tertio anno ovat et nidum facit iuxta aquas et multum diligit pullos et acriter pugnat pro eis' (This bird lays eggs in its third year. It makes its nest near water and greatly cares for its young. It fights fiercely for them).[49] All this is true. Swans nest in their third year and are attentive parents. Their fighting stance is well known and termed 'busking'.[50]

Albertus appears to be describing the Mute Swan. One clue is in his description of the swan as 'est autem mali gressus et bonae natationis et mediocris volatus' (a poor walker, an excellent swimmer, and a mediocre flyer).[51]

The Mute Swan, writes ornithologist Cramp, 'looks more graceful on water [...] but on land moves more slowly and clumsily with waddling gait'.[52] Another clue is in his description that: 'Pede uno natat et alium elevat et ponit supra versus caudam' (It swims with one foot and it elevates the other, and it places it above, near the tail) – true of the Mute Swan.[53] Albertus' account of the swan is one of the richest in medieval literature because it is saturated in details derived from observation.

Other writers combined Aristotelian observation with allegory. Albertus' student Thomas Aquinas (d. 1274) describes the swan's neck: the swan 'longo collo quod habet ex profunditate terrae vel aquae cibum trahit (with its long neck brings up food from deep down in the ground or water).[54] This is true: in fact, the swan's neck has more vertebrae than any other known species (including the giraffe) and its length is instrumental in increasing its feeding radius.[55] The swan's neck, Aquinas says, symbolises those who seek gain by appearing just. Allegorical and observation methodologies combine.

THE SWAN'S SONG

The most recorded feature of the swan across medieval natural history is its song. In his one-line summaries of birds in *Plaint of Nature* (twelfth century), Alan of Lille writes, 'Illic olor, sui funeris praeco, mellitae citharizationis organo vitae vaticinabatur apocopam' (Here the swan, herald of his own death, foretold the ending of his life with sounds of honeyed musicality).[56] Bestiaries too, put it glibly: 'Sed et in extremis cum cignus moritur, valde dulciter moriens canere perhibetur' (But when at length the swan dies, it sings very sweetly).[57] Vincent of Beauvais (thirteenth century) describes the swan as the singer at his own funeral ('cantatur cignus funeris ipse sui').[58] Thomas of Cantimpré, echoing sentiments in the *Phaedo*, writes that the swan dies singing joyfully ('Naturaliter preit mortem suam in cantu letitie et iubilationis moriturus').[59] Albertus also focuses on the swan's song. While he had not witnessed that Hyperborean swans sing when humans played instruments, he does tell us: 'Sed quod expertum est aput nos, est quod non concinunt nisi tempore doloris et tristitiae' (But what is experienced among us is that they sing only in time of pain and sorrow).[60] Albertus filters historical records against experience. Intriguingly, he attests to hearing swans sing. The swan is further tied to its song in medieval astronomy. The constellation 'cygnus' (swan) sits directly next to the constellation 'lyra' (lyre). The swan's connection with its song is even written in the stars (Figure 2).[61]

Thomas of Cantimpré explores the causes behind the swan's death song and states that this is due to a feather: 'Instante morte pennam in cerebro figit et sic dulciter canit' (Approaching death, it pierces a feather into its brain, and so it sings sweetly).[62] Variations on this idea appear in the writings of Bartholomaeus Anglicus, Vincent of Beauvais, Brunetto Latini, and John Gower.[63] McCulloch explains that this likely derives from Ovid's *Fasti*, which states: 'Flebilibus numeris veluti canentia dura / traiectus penna tempora cantat olor' (Such notes as the swan chants in mournful numbers when the cruel shaft has pierced his snowy brow).[64] Ovid's 'penna' (feather) seems to be a literary expression for an arrow ('feathered arrow' or 'shaft'). This was later

Figure 2: *Miniature of Holor, or the Swan, 1475–1480. New York, New York Public Library, Spencer Collection, MS 28, fig. 8. New York Public Library. This is a late medieval representation of the constellation 'cygnus' or swan. The line of stars represents the swan's wingspan. The constellation 'cygnus' sits next to the constellation 'lyra', associating swans with music even in the stars.*

translated literally as the swan's own 'penna' (pinion and feathers) piercing its brain to unlock its death song. It also might be the origin behind the phrase 'feather-brain'.

The persistent attestations to the swan's song are puzzling.[65] Classical and medieval writers likely encountered the Mute Swan. The Mute Swan – with its orange bill and distinct, curved neck – is portrayed on classical vases and coins.[66] Burial remains identify the Mute Swan in Europe from at least the Roman period.[67] The Mute Swan's prevalence and voicelessness contrasts starkly against the many references to the swan's song. This creates dissonance between written record and eye-witness accounts. Bitterli describes this conundrum as the swan's 'striking antithesis of silence and sound'.[68] This juxtaposition between historical record and experience resulted in creative explanations that enabled the Mute Swan to sing.

For centuries the Mute Swan has provided a poignant tension between voice and voicelessness. For both classical and medieval writers, the swan's song was interpreted through distinctive features of the Mute Swan. Riddle 7 of the Old English Exeter Book describes a creature silent on land, but musical in flight. The final lines of the Riddle provide its identifying clue:

> Frætwe mine
> swogað hlude ond swinsiað,
> torhte singað, þonne ic getenge ne beom
> flode ond foldan, ferende gæst.

My adornments sound loudly and make melody, sing clearly, when I am not resting on water and land, a travelling spirit.[69]

The key clue to the Riddle is that the adornments 'torhte singað' (sing clearly) in flight.[70] Unlike the northern swan, the Mute Swan has wing-beats that produce a distinctive sound. This is described by ornithologists as a 'loud, penetrating, rhythmic singing sound resembling "vaou-vaou-vaou"', audible within a mile radius.[71] These wing-beats keep the swans together during flight, replacing the function of the voice. Ornithologists call them the Mute Swan's 'singing wings'.[72] The Mute Swan's distinctive wing-beats have been recorded as the swan's song since Antiquity. The *Homeric Hymn* states, 'even the swan sings in praise of you [Apollo], / with the clear sound of its beating wings'.[73] Aristophanes replicates the swan's wing-beats in poetic form: 'With such strains did the swans – / tio-tio-tio-tio-tynx – / beating their wings in harmonious chorus hail Apollo'.[74] In the fourth century, Gregory of Nazianzus describes swans as those whose wings raise music to Zephyrus.[75] While the Mute Swan may not sing with its throat, its wingbeats have frequently been referred to as song. Classical and medieval writers solve the conundrum of the Mute Swan's silence by describing the sound of its wings as song, linking two incongruous pieces of data.

Another example of the tension between the swan's voice and voicelessness can be seen in one of the most beautiful liturgical pieces of the Middle Ages, *Clangam, filii*. Also known as 'The Swan Sequence' or 'The Swan's Lament', this early Carolingian piece (*c*.850) begins with an invocation:

1. Clangam, filii,	I shall cry out, my sons,
ploratione una	in a lament
2a. Alitis cygni,	of the swan that winged
Qui transfretavit aequora.	its way across the oceans.[76]

The song shifts to the persona of a swan who has been buffeted on the ocean by storms, so much so that flight and food are impossible. In the face of death ('Intuens mortifera', 5a), the swan prays for deliverance, for stars to appear – a sure sign of a calming storm. The swan's prayers are answered with the arrival of 'rutila […] aurora' (red dawn, 7a). A particularly Christian symbol of hope, the new dawn enables the swan to fly to land, whereupon she entreats all the birds to sing 'Regi magno sit gloria' ('Glory be to the great king', 10).

Clangam, filii evokes a number of swan associations. It opens in lament. It reinforces the idea that swans only sing in times of pain or sorrow.[77] The song also connects to the notion that swan's sing just before their death. Once saved, it raises its voice in jubilous chorus to God, recalling classical swans that sing joyfully to Apollo.

The swan and its song have been subjected to many readings. The most persuasive, I find, is the swan as an allegory of the Christian soul.[78] Patristic texts, Carolingian sources, early vernacular literature, and bestiaries all used the bird as an image to describe the Christian soul.[79] This depiction is further supported by a single line from an early copyist (*c*.950) who interprets *Clangam, filii*, as the allegory of the Fall of mankind ('allegoria ac de cigno ad lapsum hominis').[80] The swan's plea resonates with several of the Psalms. Psalm 30 mirrors *Clangam, filii*'s sequence of woe, fear of sure death, desperate plea, deliverance, and song of praise. The swan's help at dawn is reminiscent of Psalm 46, 'God will help her at break of day'. Psalm 107 tells of merchants overwhelmed by a storm, and of their prayers, deliverance, and subsequent praise. As in the Psalms, *Clangam, filii* clearly moves from death to deliverance.

Designed to be sung, its melody was widely used in Church liturgies for over two centuries *c*.850–*c*.1100, for example, in the Celebration of Holy Innocents (eleventh century) and the Whitsun Sequence (twelfth century) (Figure 3).[81] As much of the poem is written in the swan's

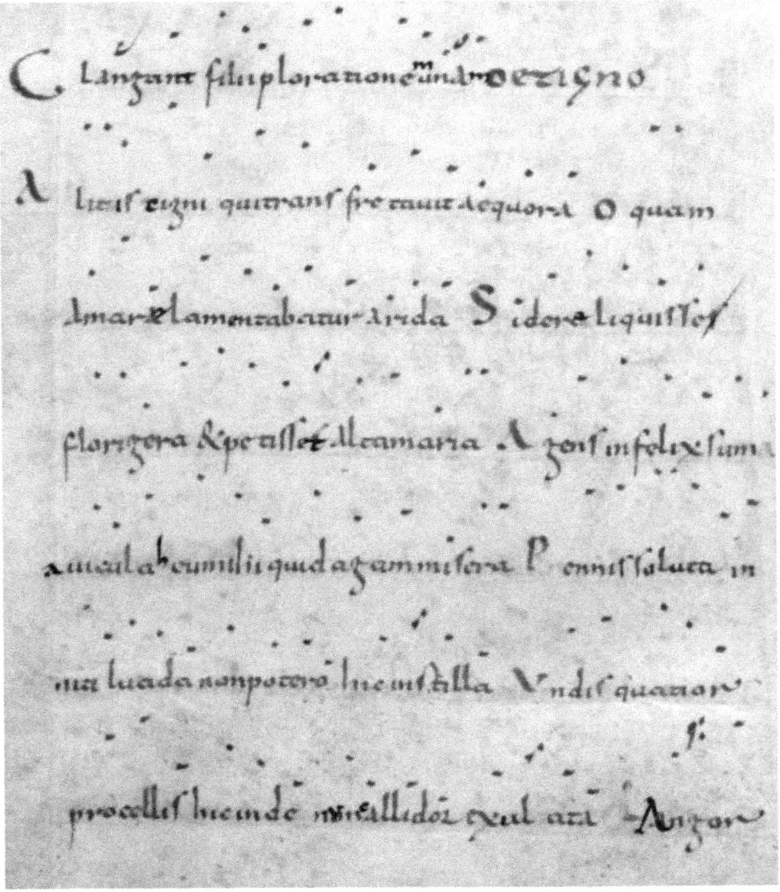

Figure 3: Clingam, filii *in musical notation, c.975–1010. Paris, Bibliothèque nationale de France, MS Latin, 1084, fol. 280r. Public domain. The dots above the words represent musical notes and was meant to be sung. As this song is written from the swan's perspective, human voice enables the swan to metaphorically 'sing'.*

first-person, *Clangam, filii* provides the swan with a voice. Those singing *Clangam, filii* adopt the swan's persona, and become human conduits through whom the swan can sing. Moreover, swan bones were used as medieval flutes, enabling the swan to sing after its death.[82] Human artistry has supplied the swan with song.

MARVELLOUS POSSIBILITIES

Medieval records place the Mute Swan between sound and silence. Its song was rendered through its wings and through haunting strains of human music. But other explanations exist for the universal reference to the swan's song. Two other breeds of swan inhabit Europe: the Whooper Swan and Bewick's Swan. Both are known for their vociferous musicality, especially in winter, when they group in hundreds, even thousands. Bewick's Swans produce, in the words of Cramp, 'a musical babble of shorter, less trumpeting notes'; their voices are 'used extensively, year-round, individually and in chorus, especially on water and in flight'.[83] The Whooper Swan's call is loud, writes Cramp, with 'musical trumpet or bugle-like quality, deeper and stronger than Bewick's Swan'.[84] The Whooper's strength of sound stems from its atypical anatomy. It has an extra loop of trachea within the sternum.[85] With the Whooper in mind, Isidore's remark about the strength of the swan's song stemming from its sternum appears to be remarkably accurate. These northern singing swans may explain the many medieval and classical references to the singing swan.

Other parts of Isidore's swan description may have basis in truth. For example, Isidore mentions swans singing in Hyperborean regions. In classical texts the 'Hyperboreas' was the land beyond the North-Wind (Boreas), now thought to refer to Arctic regions.[86] The two European breeds of swans that are known to inhabit the Arctic are the Whooper Swan and Bewick's Swan. Both swans nest in the Tundra and Arctic and undertake extensive migrations to winter in Britain and along the Baltic Coast. If their migration and distribution patterns have remained similar over time, perhaps this lends credence to Isidore's record of Hyperborean swans.[87] Moreover as both swans sing in winter, when they inhabit northern Europe, it may have been possible for medieval writers, such as Albertus, not only to see these swans, but to hear them sing.

Isidore also records that these Hyperborean swans sing along to human instruments. Both northern swans are known to sing in duets. Their voice, Cramp writes, is 'quite powerful, sonorous, and often musical in northern *Cygnus* (in which [it is] sometimes used in pair duet)'.[88] Singing to human voice and instrument is a feature of songbirds. Pet parakeets are known to accompany human songs. This is possible because songbirds and humans share the same 'singing gene' – a trait that speech pathologists often employ when analysing human speech performance.[89] Northern swans are known to sing duets and have the genetic capacity to sing to human song, supporting Isidore's statement.

Medieval writers certainly believed this to be true. Plate 1 depicts swans singing to the lyre. Note the swan's black bill and straighter neck, features reminiscent of Bewick's and Whooper Swans – both known for their musicality and Arctic habitation. Medieval statements of swans harmonising to human music may reference a truth about northern swans, perhaps one that has been lost in technological advances – of diesel engines, jet aircrafts, and radars – that have altered human relationships with nature: that those living in the Middle Ages inhabited a world with a nearness to nature that has been lost to us. Considering their musicality, northern location, and ability to harmonise, Bewick's or Whooper Swans seem to match Isidore's description.

But the remaining question is whether or not swans sing when they die. The modern emphasis of natural history relies on observation, empirical data, and widespread similarities across genus and species.[90] Nearly the exact opposite is true of medieval writings. Early views of medieval natural history were certain that the earth's creatures, situated within a heavenly cosmos, contained marvellous properties. Medieval natural history emphasised a creature's marvellous abilities as the most important feature it possessed. For the swan it was its song, prophetic and heightened in beauty, that heralded its own death.

While this is by no means a widespread occurrence, some, limited, evidence does exist for this phenomenon. The Whooper Swan's extra loop of trachea may provide partial explanation.[91] 'Prolonged exhalation of air from [the] trachea in [a] dying bird', Cramp writes, 'can produce a series of musical notes, probably accounting for [the] legend of [the] "Swan-song"'.[92] Of the Whooper, Witherby stipulates: 'Legend of song of dying swan has some basis in this species, the final expiration of air from [its] long convoluted wind-pipe producing a wailing, flute-like sound given out quite slowly',[93] while, according to Arnott, the dying song of the Whooper was first attested to by Peter Pallas in Russia.[94] The same feature has been noted in other Tundra

Swans with convoluted trachea.[95] The famous ornithologist, D. G. Elliot witnessed this same phenomenon in the Whistling Swan:

> On receiving his wound the wings became fixed and he commenced at once his song, which was continued until the water was reached, nearly half a mile away. I am perfectly familiar with every note a Swan is accustomed to utter, but never before nor since have I heard any like those sung by this stricken bird. Most plaintive in character and musical in tone, it sounded at times like the soft running of the notes in an octave [...] and as the sound was borne to us, mellowed by the distance, we stood astonished, and could only exclaim, 'We have heard the song of the dying Swan'.[96]

Both ornithologists and academics support the possibility of the swan's death song. Wilmore writes, 'the legend that before a swan dies it sings a beautiful farewell has been discovered to be true in the case of the Whistling Swan'.[97] The legend, Arnott argues, 'turns out to be precisely accurate in all its details'.[98] H. Rackham comments on Pliny's disbelief of the swan's dying song. He notes, 'the story is true of the Whooper Swan but not of the ordinary Mute Swan'.[99] The swan's song, attested to by medieval authors, observed by eyewitnesses, and recorded by ornithologists and scholars, is both biologically and genetically possible. Taken as an exceptional and rare possibility, the swan's dying song is one more of the swan's marvellous features recorded by Isidore that has the capacity to be true.

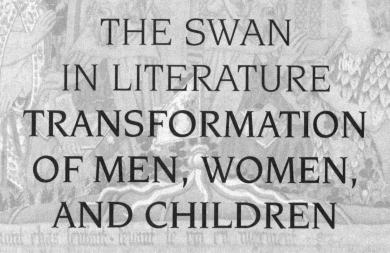

THE SWAN
IN LITERATURE
TRANSFORMATION
OF MEN, WOMEN,
AND CHILDREN

THROUGHOUT MEDIEVAL literature the swan is typified by its transformation. Medieval precedent drew upon classical accounts of men transforming into swans. The most well-known trope is that of the swan-maiden, but contrary to expectation, her presence is infrequent in medieval literature. However, the topos of children transforming into swans recurs often and links explicitly to tales of the Knight of the Swan.

MALE TRANSFORMATION

Leda and the Swan

The story is well known: Jupiter transforms into a swan to sleep with the mortal Leda, thereby fathering semi-mortal children. It is recorded by Homer, Euripides, Apollodorus, and Pindar, but the story made its way into the Middle Ages through Ovid and Fulgentius.[1] In Ovid's *Metamorphoses*, the reference to Jupiter and Leda is brief: in her weaving Arachne 'fecit olorinis Ledam recubare sub alis' (wrought Leda, beneath the swan's wings).[2] Ovid also mentions Leda as the wife of Tyndareus and the mother of twins – Castor and Pollux.[3] She is also thought to have given birth to Helen of Troy.

The stories of Ovid were initially carried into the Middle Ages through Fulgentius (fifth to sixth century

AD). Fulgentius gives the merest bones of the narrative of Leda and Jupiter: that Jupiter disguised himself as a swan and slept with Leda, who laid eggs from which were born Castor, Pollux, and Helen of Troy. Fulgentius interprets Jupiter as a symbol of power. He derives the swan's meaning from its name. Because the Latin 'olor' (swan) is similar to 'oliguria' (associated with insults), Fulgentius interprets the swan as something insulting or lowly.[4] Thus Jupiter's power is tainted by his transformation into a swan. For him the story's moral is that 'Omnis potentia injuriae mixta, speciem suae generositatis mutat' (All power getting involved with insults changes the appearance of its magnanimity).[5] Power is sullied, the adulterous liaison is sordid, and the offspring symbolises pride and evil.

The story of Leda and the Swan was extremely popular and well represented in classical art. Many images depict the act of copulation – the swan grasping Leda's neck, which reflects the cob's natural mating stance.[6] At its most benign, the story of Leda and the Swan was seen as a tale of passionate lovers. At its most extreme it was a celebration of bestiality – even bestial rape. Frequently the story was viewed as highly erotic, the element of rape often overlooked to celebrate the transgressive, the deviant, and the pornographic.[7] From the Renaissance, Leda and the Swan has been a favourite artistic theme consistently reworked by the Great Masters. As Ovid's works began to be translated, the story's deviant escapades required reworking for its Christian audience.

Christian authors performed intellectual backflips in order to draw spiritual meaning from Ovid's works.

The *Ovide Moralisé*, a fourteenth-century French adaptation and allegory of Ovid's work, offers two interpretations of Leda and the Swan. Perhaps influenced by Fulgentius, the first interpretation views Jupiter as the personification of power and Leda's rape as injustice ('D'iniure et de poissance ensamble'), signifying abusive power over the lowly.[8]

The second interpretation is slightly more shocking: Jupiter's transformation into a swan signifies Christ's transformation into mortal flesh.

> Nostre Diex et nostre sauverres,
> Se mist en samblance de cigne,
> Qui voire humilité designe

> Our God and our saviour
> Made himself into the form of a swan
> Which signifies true humility.[9]

Unlike the proud swan of the bestiary, Christ as swan is humble. The shame and insults ('honte et laidure') Christ received whilst transformed are reminiscent of Fulgentius' shameful and lowly swan.[10] And like Plato's dying swan, Christ suffered his death with joy.

> Si s'apresta ioieusement
> De venir a sa mortel paine,
> Si com li cignes, qui demaine
> Grant ioie et trop s'envoise et chante,
> Quant sa mort voit venir presante.

> And prepared himself joyously
> To come to his final suffering
> Like the swan, which makes
> Great joy and greatly rejoices and sings
> When it sees its death approaching.[11]

'For the joy set before him he [Christ] endured the cross, scorning its shame', writes the author of the book of Hebrews (12:2).

To the medieval mind, Jupiter provided a clear parallel with Christ: for love, a deity transforms. In medieval theology, Christ willingly subjected himself to transformation – from God to human – to redeem mankind.[12] After the twelfth century, Christ's transformative ability was occasionally emphasised in shocking ways.[13] The *Ovide Moralisé* has taken a story of bestiality and likened it to Christ's incarnation.

Cycnus, Cycnus, Cycnus

Swan transformation is not only consigned to Jupiter. A handful of men – all named Cycnus – transform into swans in classical literature. Ovid mentions three, but others exist.[14] Ovid's first Cycnus deeply mourns the death of Phaethon and abandons his kingdom of Liguria to grieve for his friend. Perhaps because he resembles the mourning swan, Cycnus is transformed into his namesake:

> digitosque ligat iunctura rubentis,
> penna latus velat, tenet os sine acumine rostrum.
> fit nova Cycnus avis.

> And a web-like membrane joined his reddened fingers,
> wings clothed his sides, and a blunt beak became his
> mouth. So Cycnus became a strange new bird – the swan.[15]

Like the lamenting swan, Cycnus grieves, which in this case
likely has homoerotic undertones. Cycnus' name and con-
tinual sorrow seem to prefigure his final swan form.

Ovid's second Cycnus is a boy – son of Apollo and loved
by Phylius. Annoyed with Phylius' advances, Cycnus sets
Phylius impossible tasks, but when Phylius fulfils them,
Cycnus spurns each gift. Angered, Phylius withholds the
last gift. Intending his death to rebuke Phylius, Cycnus
impetuously leaps from a cliff: 'Factus olor niveis pendebat
in aere pennis' (But changed to a swan he remained floating
in the air on snowy wings).[16] In a second display of unful-
filled – and here unrequited – homoerotic love, this Cycnus
is saved by his father Apollo, further cementing Apollo's
associations with swans.

Ovid's third Cycnus is the son of Poseidon who battles Achilles in the Trojan War. Both are sons of gods and
endowed with supernatural protection. Finding Cycnus
impervious to sword and spear, Achilles strangles him.
Before he can plunder Cycnus' body, it vanishes: 'Corpus
deus aequoris albam contulit in volucrem, cuius modo
nomen habebat' (For the god has changed the body into
the white bird whose name he lately bore).[17] Poseidon has
intervened and changed his son into a swan. This story
is only recorded by Ovid, says Martin.[18] It evidences the
(im)mortal tension between two demigods. For all three
characters, their names appear to influence their transformed form.[19]

Of Ovid's Cycnuses, the story of Cycnus and Phaethon seems to be the one most frequently retold, appearing in both medieval French and English moralised tales. Caxton's fifteenth-century translation emphasises Cycnus' lack of pride in forsaking his realm 'to lyue sewrly in pourete' (to live visibly in poverty).[20] This humble swan is the foil to the proud, rich swan found in bestiaries. The comparison is nearly explicit, for Caxton writes, 'Onto Cynus shold be compared the ryche men that meke & humble them self'.[21] Caxton's meek swan provides the antidote to the bestiary swan's vices of wealth and pride.

Caxton's *The Booke of Ovyde* also briefly relates the story of Leda, as well as that of Cycnus the son of Poseidon. In Caxton's story, Achilles only 'fonde the body naked of the sowle, whych thenne Neptunus had transformed in to a whyte fowle named a swane, whyche yet beryth the name that he had to fore'.[22] Here the swan is Cycnus' soul, departed from his body, and not bodily metamorphosis. This reinforces the idea of birds as symbols of human souls in medieval literature.[23]

Apart from these Ovidian references, the trope of male transformation into swans occurs rarely in medieval literature. The knight in Marie de France's *Yonec* transforms into a hawk, offering himself as faery paramour to a lady imprisoned by her jealous husband.[24] But, by and large, in medieval literature, swan-transformations into men are often connected to Ovid.

SWAN-MAIDENS

Scholarship frequently refers to medieval accounts of swan-maidens. A common motif, 'swan-maidens' are defined in the Oxford English Dictionary as 'supernatural maidens having the power of transforming themselves into swans by means of a robe of swan's feathers or of a magic ring or chain'.[25] The trope of the swan-maid has been viewed as a central presence in medieval literature, notably catalogued by Stith Thompson in his folklore index.[26] Thompson defines the motif through male agency: the knight usually 'seizes one of the swan coats and will not return it to the maiden unless she agrees to marry him'.[27] Schofield comparatively analysed three medieval texts featuring swan-maidens: the Old Norse *Völundarkviða* (ninth century), the Middle High German *Friedrich von Schwaben* (fourteenth century), and the Old French *Graelent* (twelfth century).[28] The following section argues that although swan-maidens recur commonly in scholarly criticism, very few accounts exist in medieval literature.[29]

Völundarkviða
The earliest medieval reference to a swan-maiden occurs in the Old Norse *Völundarkviða*, written in skaldic verse. The poem reads:

Meyiar flugo sunnan	Maidens flew from the south
Myrkvið í gögnom,	through Mirkwood,
alvítr unga(r),	foreign beings, young,
ørlög drýgia.	their fate to fulfil.
Þær á sævar strönd	They by a lake's shore
settuz at hvílaz,	settled to rest themselves,
drósir suðrœnar,	southern damsels,
dýrt lín spunno.	precious linen they spun.

2.

Ein nam þeira	One of them took
Egil at veria,	Egill to cherish,
fögr mær fira,	lovely maid of the living,
faðmi liósom.	on her shining breast.
Önnur um Slagfinn	The second over Slagfiðr
svanfiaðrar dró,	drew her swan's wings,
en in þriðia,	while the third,
þeira systir,	sister of these,
varði hvítan	enfolded the fair-white
háls Völundar.	neck of Völundr.[30]

These verses portray swan-maidens who choose three men to love: one takes Egill; another Slagfiðr; a third enfolds the neck of Völundr. Of these women, Dronke writes: 'They themselves draw their chosen husbands to them.'[31] Alaric Hall demonstrates the agency is with the swan-women.[32] Their transformative nature is indicated through 'svan-fiaðrar' (swan's feathers). The nature of transformation is enigmatic, seemingly involving cloaks, but possibly inherent. Imitating migratory patterns of birds, who too nest and depart, these women fly off, never to be recovered by their eternally disconsolate hubands. Unlike in Thompson's definition, the men neither steal their cloaks, nor are they rediscovered, enabling the women to escape. Their motives for leaving, in the words of McKinnell, are 'inscrutable to human beings'.[33] This Old Norse text appears to set the precedent for swan-maidens throughout the Middle Ages.

Friedrich von Schwaben, Graelent, and Guingamor

Next in Schofield's list of swan-maidens is *Friedrich von Schwaben*. *Friedrich* is the story of the eponymous knight, separated from his beloved Angelbury, who has been transformed by a witch into a white dove.[34] To break the enchantment, Friedrich is instructed to wait by a mountain for three doves to alight, steal their clothing, and persuade one of them to marry him: 'So komment dry tuben her geflogen / (Haimlich sitz vertrogen), / Und sy ziechent ab ir gewand' (Thus three doves will come flying / Sit secretly, discreetly / And they will take off their garments).[35] Through the aid of a herb that renders him invisible, Friedrich does so, and he and Angelbury are reunited. The women's transformation is enabled by removing their clothing. Schofield calls *Friedrich von Schwaben*, 'a romantic version of the story of Wayland and the swan-maidens'.[36] But it is worth emphasising that in the *Friedrich* manuscripts, no swans appear. The women change into white birds, but they are doves, not swans.

The third text in Schofield's swan-maiden typology is *Graelent*. The knight Graelent stumbles upon a fountain where a beautiful woman bathes. He seizes her clothing, and through coercion, the woman becomes his paramour, on condition that he keeps her stipulated interdict. While the woman certainly wields supernatural powers, there is no mention that she transforms, either into a bird or a swan. Her clothes are not bird-garments, merely 'sa vesteüre' (her vestments).[37]

The Old French *Guingamor* (late twelfth century) has also been identified as a swan-maiden tale.[38] Yet no swans appear in this text either. Pursing a boar, Guingamor comes across a beautiful woman bathing. He hides her clothes in the hollow of an oak tree so that she may not escape. These are merely clothes ('dras'), not transformative bird-feathers.[39] Nor does she transform.

While stealing a woman's clothes as she bathes seems to indicate coercion over a supernatural paramour, no swan appears in *Friedrich*, *Guingamor*, or *Graelent*. In *Friedrich* alone does a woman transform – Angelbury into a dove. Although these texts are said to epitomise swan-maiden typologies, none features a swan-maiden.[40]

Other Versions

Closer to the mark is the twelfth-century Latin *Dolopathos* (*c.*1190). Chasing a white stag, a king encounters a lady bathing, clutching a gold chain. The king seizes her chain and they become paramours. Twice the text refers to this lady as 'nimpha', and she immediately foretells she will give birth to septuplets.[41] All the children are born with costly chains about their necks, and when these necklaces are removed, the children transform into swans. While the nymph-queen herself never transforms into a swan, she does give birth to children who do. The text hints at, but never exposes, her transformative swan potential.

A similar story is told in the *Elioxe* version of *La Naissance du Chevalier au Cygne* (twelfth century). Meeting at a fountain, a knight and a maiden called Elioxe marry. Elioxe foretells she will die giving birth to septuplets.[42] Elioxe's subsequent death curtails enquiry into her transformative nature. The text does call her 'la fee' (fay), and her children, born with necklaces, can transform into swans.[43] However, her supernatural abilities are not emphasised, nor does she transform into a swan.

In the *Beatrix* version of *La Naissance* the queen is neither nymph nor faery. Queen Beatrice slanders a mother of twins, believing it evidence of adultery.[44] In divine punishment,

God impregnates her with septuplets.[45] While the children are born with costly necklaces and have the ability to turn into swans, there is no indication that their mother can transform into a swan or is of faery origin.

Irish

Plenty of Irish accounts involve swans, but these appear to be less well known across medieval Europe. In the *Children of Lir* (twelfth century), an evil stepmother transforms the king's children into swans.[46] In *Aislinge Oengusso* (twelfth century), Oengus identifies his beloved, transformed into a swan apart from all the other birds.[47] He too transforms into a swan and they reunite. In *Tochmarc Emire*, Cú Chulainn wounds a flying swan, but realising it is the woman Derbforgaill, he attempts to save her. In the process he tastes her blood, condemning them to be star-crossed lovers.[48] Medieval Irish literature on swans is thus more varied, featuring women who do transform into swans, but they do not circulate widely in European vernacular contexts and appear to have little influence on the medieval perception of swan-maidens.

Prose *Völundarkviða*

Accompanying the ninth-century poetic *Völundarkviða* is a short introduction in prose dating to the fourteenth century. Incorporated later, the prose adaptation adds significant changes regarding the agency of the swan women.

> Snemma of morgin fundo þeir á vazströndo konor þriár, ok spunno lín. Þar vóro hiá þeim álptarhamir þeira; þat vóro valkyrior. [...] Þeir höfðo þær heim til skála með

sér. Fekk Egill Ölrúnar, en Slagfiðr Svanhvítar, en Völundr Alvítrar. Þau biöggo siau vetr. Þá flugu þær at vitia víga ok kvómo eigi aptr.

In the early morning they found on the lake-shore three women, and they were spinning linen. There lay beside them their swan-garments; they were valkryies. [...] They took them to their house with them. Egill took Ölrún as his wife, and Slagfiðr Svanhvít, and Völundr Alvítr. They lived together for seven winters. Then the wives flew away to seek battles and did not come back.[49]

Key variations occur in the prose. The first is that female agency, so strong in the Skaldic verse, is almost totally diminished. Here the grammar places the men as active agents taking the women. The second is that the women have shape-shifting garments called 'álptarhamir'. The term 'hamir' is integral to Old Norse conceptions of shape-shifting.[50] A third change is that the women are explicitly described as valkyries ('valkyrior'). Their role as valkyries explains their departure 'to seek battle'. Valkyries appear as swans in other Old Norse texts, further linking swan-maidens to valkyries.[51]

None of these texts fulfil Thompson's swan-maiden typology.[52] In both accounts of *Völundarkviða*, the women are never captured, coerced into marriage, or deprived of their swan-garments. Although typified as 'swan-maidens', the women in *Friedrich*, *Graelent*, and *Guingamor* do not transform into swans. Instead the term 'swan-maiden' has been assimilated into a larger typology regarding faery paramours. In other texts, women give birth to swan-children, but do not themselves transform. Apart from Irish accounts, which appear to have little direct connection to the other European vernaculars, the swan-maiden only exists in Old Norse accounts. The medieval swan-maiden appears to be just as elusive as the swan's dying song.

SWAN CHILDREN

More frequent than swan-maidens in medieval literature is the presence of swan children. One of the earliest references to swan children is the Old Irish *Fate of the Children of Lir* (*c.*twelfth century).[53] Comprising two sets of twins, the children of King Lir are transformed into swans by their evil stepmother using a druidical wand. The children wander on lakes for centuries until St Mochaomhóg delivers them, placing silver chains around their necks and setting them on a holy altar. When a henchman steals them from the altar and removes their chains, they transform into old, withered humans – all but dust. The saint quickly baptises them and they die – seemingly preserved by Providence until they can be given Christian burial.

Knight of the Swan

While the *Children of Lir* was not widely translated throughout medieval Europe, aspects of the story are present in one of the most important traditions of swan children in medieval literature – *Le Chevalier au Cygne* or the Knight of the Swan ('miles cigni'). Tales such as *La Chanson du Chevalier au Cygne et de Godefroi de Bouillon* (*c.*twelfth century) tell the legend of a knight who is drawn in a boat by a swan.[54] He defends a maiden in trial by combat, and upon his success they wed on one condition: that she must not enquire into his origins. When she breaks this interdict, the swan arrives, and the knight departs whence he came. The Swan Knight was alleged to be the grandfather of Godfrey of Bouillon, ruler of Jerusalem (1109–10). As the Swan Knight and Godfrey grew in popularity, explanations emerged as to why the Swan Knight is accompanied by a swan.

The oldest extant tale is *Dolopathos*. Mentioned previously, a knight marries a nymph who gives birth to septuplets, all born with costly chains (Plate 2). Jealous, the queen-mother incriminates her son's bride, substituting babies for puppies, signifying both adultery and bestiality. The queen is punished by being half-buried. Though meant to die, the children are instead abandoned and adopted by a hermit.[55] Years later, the children are discovered and the chains of all but one daughter are stolen, consigning the children to swan form. A blacksmith attempts to forge the chains into a goblet, but only one link of one chain is damaged. Wrongs are set right when the daughter attracts the attention of her father, relaying to him that her brothers have been transformed into swans. Under torture the queen-mother reveals all: the is queen exonerated and the chains are restored to each child, save one, whose chain was damaged. The remaining swan cannot transform into human form, but instead follows his brother on knightly exploits: 'Hic est cignus, de quo fama in eternum perseverat, quod cathena aurea militem in navicula trahat armatum' (Here is the swan, whose fame continues into eternity, because he pulls the armed knight in a ship by a gold chain) (Plate 2).[56] *Dolopathos* provides the origins for the Swan Knight as well as the reason he is accompanied by a swan, who is his transformed brother.

Elioxe and Beatrix

Other texts soon expanded upon *Dolopathos'* brief account of the Swan Knight's origins. Chief among these is the Old French Crusade Cycle, *La Naissance du Chevalier au Cygne*. Comprising at least four variations, *La Naissance* texts increase the focus on the Swan Knight. In fact, according to Mickel and Nelson each version is 'altered to varying degrees in an effort to make a closer connection with the Swan Knight branch'.[57] A few thousand lines long, the *Elioxe* version is similar in plot to *Dolopathos*. The nymph-queen dies giving birth to septuplets; her mother-in-law calumniates her, claiming she gave birth to serpents. The queen-mother's henchman abandons the children to die, but they are raised by a hermit. A courtier, on advice from the queen-mother, steals the children's chains and they transform into swans, save one sister. The king notices the girl, and through enquiry, the truth comes to light. All swans save one regain human form. This enduring consequence of maleficence – the child turned swan irreversibly, occasioned by human ill-will and the nebulous, inherent powers of the faery supernatural – causes pain to one of the swan's brothers. He says:

> Mais cil que nos laisons el vivier tant noer,
> Qui nostre germains est, il me fait molt penser;
> Je l'ainc molt, ne le puis laisier seul demorer;
> Se j'en vois jel menrai, se puis engien trover.

> But he whom we leave swimming so much on the lake,
> Who is our sibling, he gives me a good deal to think about;
> I love him dearly, and cannot leave him to remain alone;
> If I go away I will take him with me, if I can find a way.[58]

The knight is unwilling to part from his swan-brother and together they seek adventure. The story tells of 'cisne qui la nef vait a son col traiant, / Et del jentil vallet dedens sa nef gisant' (the swan which goes pulling the boat with its neck / and of the noble youth lying in his boat).[59] Thanks to their iconic pairing, the human brother becomes identified by his swan-sibling. In *Elioxe*, it is affection for his swan-brother that makes him the Knight of the Swan, the renowned Chevalier au Cygne.

The later *Beatrix* version changes the story to make the Swan Knight the central character. The narrative roughly follows the *Elioxe* in plot, but when the siblings' chains are stolen, it is not the sister who remains untransformed, but a brother – Elias. Instructed by an angel, Elias defends his mother in combat and frees all but one of his siblings from swan form. Later, an angel instructs Elias to return to his swan-brother and embark on *aventure* with him: 'Et ilueques le cisne, ton frere, trouveras' (And there you will find the swan, your brother).[60] Because Elias journeys with his swan-brother, he becomes known as the Swan Knight, his new identity orchestrated by God and girded in divine approval. Shifting from sister to brother changes the story's focus to Elias's coming-of-age – from his birth to knightly prowess. Nelson and Mickel argue that this was precisely the point: 'Aware that the story's primary purpose was to disclose the origin of the Swan Knight, the author altered the central focus of the narrative from the single daughter to one of the sons'.[61]

English Versions
The *Beatrix* version is retold in the Middle English *Chevelere Assigne* (fourteenth century). Although only 300 lines, the

English makes several expansions.[62] The first is that the Swan Knight – now called Enyas – is ignorant of basic etiquette, reminiscent of the coming-of-age story of Chrétien's Perceval (the Fair Unknown). The second expansion is the distress of the untransformed swan-sibling: 'Hit was doole forto se þe sorrow þat he made: / He bote hymself with his byll, þat all his breste bledde, / And all his feyre federes fomede upon blode' (It was sad to see the great sorrow that he made / He bit himself with his bill, so that all his breast bled / And all his fair feathers foamed with blood'.[63] The tale ends on this note of distress without mentioning the swan's future as his brother's companion. This is alluded to, obliquely, in the poem's final lines. Enyas receives a second baptism, where he is rechristened 'Chevelere Assygne' (the Knight of the Swan). His new name links Enyas, and possibly his brother to future Swan Knight identities. Yet the English text never supplies a direct link between Enyas and his swan-brother, the seeming purpose of previous tales, thereby severing a motif from its previous usage.

Although the Middle English text ends unhappily, other versions remedied this. In *La Fin d'Elias* of the Old French Crusade Cycle, the swan is handed a letter by a figure in white, which instructs that the goblets be changed into chalices and the swan placed between the chalices during mass:

> Tout droit a icele eure, si con j'oï conter,
> Que Jhesus, nostre Sire ki tout a a sauver,
> Fist le pain en l'autel ens en sa car müer
> Et le vin en son sanc pour son peule sauver,

A cele eure tout droit fist le cisne müer
El plus biel baceler que on pouist trouver.

As I heard it told, at exactly the moment in which Jesus
our Savior, who saves us all, changed the bread on the
altar into his flesh and the wine into his blood in order
to save his people, at that moment the swan turned
immediately into the most beautiful young man one
could find.[64]

The story changes only slightly in Copland's History of Helyas
(1515). Instructed in a dream, his mother Bewtris orders the
goblets be changed into chalices, placed upon an altar, and
that the swan laid between them during mass. Surrounded
by the prayers of his family, at the moment the bread
transforms into the body of Christ, the 'swanne retourned
into his propre fourme and was a man'.[65] Drawing on powerful transformations embedded within the framework
of Christian ritual, in both texts the swan becomes man.
Christian power triumphs.

THE KNIGHT OF THE SWAN

Wolfram von Eschenbach

Circulating around the same time as stories of swan-
children were the legends of the Swan Knight, particularly
prominent in medieval German literature. Wolfram von
Eschenbach (thirteenth century) incorporated the Swan
Knight into his retelling of Chrétien de Troyes' Arthurian
romance. His romance ends with Parzival's son, Lohengrin,
becoming the Swan Knight.[66] The princess of Brabant, surrounded by a crowd of suitors, declares she will only marry

the man God sends her. God answers her prayer by sending her Lohengrin (Figure 4): 'Den der swane brâhte / unt des ir got gedhâte. / Z'Antwerp wart er ûz gezogen' (Destined for her by God, he [Lohengrin] was brought by the Swan and taken ashore at Antwerp).[67] Lohengrin marries her on condition that she does not ask where he is from. When she breaks this taboo, he departs with the swan to the realm of the Grail. Unlike in the French texts, the swan does not appear to be the sibling of the Swan Knight, but a divine agent.

Figure 4: *Knight of the Swan, early sixteenth century. Oxford, Bodleian Library, MS Douce 276, fol. 95r. © Bodleian Libraries, University of Oxford. CC-BY-NC 4.0. One of many medieval renditions of the swan pulling the Swan Knight in a boat.*

By ending his Arthurian romance with the legend of the Swan Knight, Wolfram fuses two disparate traditions. The Swan Knight becomes Arthurian.

Lohengrin

An extensive account of the Knight of the Swan appears in the Middle High German *Lohengrin* (thirteenth century). The Swan Knight's mysterious origins are explained by his residence in the Grail Castle alongside Arthur and his knights.[68] Writing on the Grail summons Lohengrin to defend Elsam of Brabant in judicial combat following an unjust accusation. A swan immediately appears to take Lohengrin to his destination (Figure 5). Here the swan is not a sibling, but an angel.[69] Although disguised, the swan momentarily shifts shape allowing a hermit to glimpse its true identity:

> Des abtes heilic leben rein
> schuof, daz im der swan in engels bilde erschein. [...]
> zehant er wider in vogels bilde sich wandelt.
> Der abt stuont ûf, doch het er wol gesehn daz grôze zeichen.

> The pure and holy being of the abbot meant that the swan appeared to him in the form of an angel. [...] At that instant, it turned back into the form of a bird. The abbot arose, but he had seen the great sign well.[70]

The Swan Knight's swan has changed from a sibling, whose human form has been usurped by magical powers, to an angel divinely appointed to direct and sustain the hero.

Significantly, Lohengrin wears a swan on his crest and badge, which is:

Figure 5: *Lohengrin greets the court after his arrival*, 1460. Heidelberg, Universitätsbibliothek, Cod. Pal. germ. 345, fol. 18v. Public domain. *The Swan Knight dressed in armour arrives to defend Elsam. The swan inside the boat provides the knight's identity as the Swan Knight.*

Nâch dem swan, der über sê in brâht in einer barken,
alsô ein swan stuont hie enbor
in der barken ûf dem helm.

In the form of the swan that brought him across the sea
in a boat, a swan stood tall in the boat on his helmet.[71]

Just as Chrétien's Yvain becomes the Knight of the Lion, Lohengrin has come to be identified by the animal who

Figure 6: *Lohengrin departs in a boat*, 1460. Heidelberg, Universitätsbibliothek, Cod. Pal. germ. 345, fol. 180v. Public domain. *Lohengrin departs to the realm of the Grail, ferried by the swan. Elsam appears to faint at the Swan Knight's departure.*

accompanies him. Unlike its analogues, in *Lohengrin* the hero had intended to tell his wife of his origin: 'Mîn sicherheit / sî des pfant, daz ez dâ heim iu wirt geseit / beidiu mîn nam, mîn art und mîn geslehte' (You have my word of honor that you will be told at home both my name, my heritage, and my family).[72] Her question, posed prematurely, breaks the interdict, requiring the Swan Knight to sorrowfully depart and return to the realm of the Grail (Figure 6).

Continuations

Closely derived from *Lohengrin*, the fifteenth-century Middle High German *Lorengel* provides a happier ending for the star-crossed Swan Knight and his bride. The Swan Knight, Lorengel, does not return to the Kingdom of the Grail, but instead he stays to wed Else (or Isilie), the Duchess of Brabant, and rule the duchy.[73]

The Swan Knight held particular resonance in German literature, appearing in the works of Konrad von Würzburg (thirteenth century) and Albrecht von Scharfenberg (thirteenth century). He later featured in Ulrich von Füetrer's great Arthurian saga *Buch der Abenteuer* (fifteenth century) and in Richard Wagner's famous opera, *Lohengrin*.[74]

Spin-offs and expansions of the Swan Knight legend populated medieval Europe. One variation appears in the thirteenth-century Old Norse *Karlamagnus Saga*. Another occurs in France in the *First Perceval Continuation* (*c.*1200). Pulling a boat with a golden chain, a swan delivers the corpse of the half-mortal, half-faery King Branguemuer, son of Guingamuer, to Arthur's court. The episode is cryptic, leaving much for the reader to decipher.[75] The lengthiest account of the Swan Knight's life is found in the texts of the Old French Crusade Cycle, beginning with *La Naissance*. The coverage of the Crusade Cycle is expansive. Over thousands of lines, it tells of the Swan Knight's birth, adventures, marriage, and progeny – namely Godfrey of Bouillon as well as Godfrey's own adventures. With this link to the historical Godfrey, the Swan Knight shifted from legend into history.

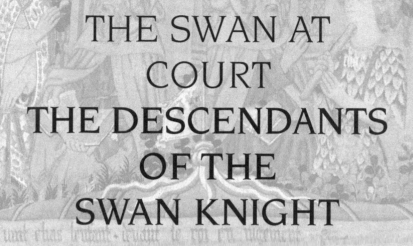

THE SWAN AT COURT
THE DESCENDANTS OF THE SWAN KNIGHT

D
URING THE Middle Ages, the image of the swan rose to unprecedented levels of popularity within the European court. Swans were depicted on shields, clerical vestments, bedding, and on the tombs of kings. Linked with nobility, and even royalty, the swan became a symbol of courtliness and soon rose to an icon of the medieval aristocracy.

COURTLY CREATURES

One of the first medieval records about swans is linked to royalty. In a charter of 966, King Edgar granted the abbots of Crowland the right to capture wild swans.[1] This indicates rights over swans were a royal prerogative. It is reputed that Richard I introduced swans into England from Cyprus on his return from the Third Crusade.[2] While this statement is almost certainly inaccurate, it not only reinforces the idea of swans as the property of kings, but also makes the king, if only mythically, responsible for the swan's very beginnings in England.

Aside from its royal connections, in early medieval Europe the swan was more generally associated with wealth and riches. The swan, and other long-necked birds, beautifully decorate long edges on items of Viking jewellery, associating swans with costly items.[3] Thus from an early date, the swan was associated with both riches and royalty.

The swan as courtly creature is reinforced by Gerald of Wales (c.1146–c.1223) in his life of St Hugh of Lincoln. On the day St Hugh was made Bishop, an unusual swan arrived at his manor. Unlike the swans known to Gerald, this swan did not have a black bill, 'quinimo locum eundem rostri planum croceoque decenter colore, una cum capite et colli parte superiore, distinctum habebat' (but instead that part of the beak was level and handsomely marked with yellow, and there was a difference, too, in the head and upper part of the neck).[4] Large in size, with a yellow beak and erect neck, it is likely this was a Whooper Swan. Attracting attention, the bird was captured and brought to the Bishop. From their first meeting, the swan was attached to St Hugh. It ate out of his hand, even nosed its head up the Bishop's sleeve, and laid its head on his breast, making low cooing sounds.

Adam of Eynsham (d. 1233) states that the swan slept in the Bishop's chambers. If anyone went by the Bishop's bed, the swan sounded a caterwaul and attacked passers-by – including Adam himself. Adam describes the swan as 'auis autem hec regia' (this royal bird), making explicit the swan's connection to royalty.[5] Iconography portrays St Hugh with his swan, which wears a golden collar amid ecclesiastical splendour (Plate 4). Pilgrims to St Hugh's shrine may have acquired a swan pilgrim badge such as featured in Figure 7.[6] A bird of kings and bishops, the swan bore a courtly reputation from the early Middle Ages.

Figure 7: *Medieval swan pilgrim badge*, c.1400–1500, *lead alloy,
1400–1500: Thames Estuary. London, British Museum, Item
No.* 1871,0714.72. © *The Trustees of the British Museum. This is
a pilgrim badge, a token for completing a pilgrimage, usually to the
shrine of a specific saint. Because it is a swan, this pilgrim badge may
be linked to St Hugh's shrine.*

GODFREY OF BOUILLON AS DESCENDED
FROM SWAN KNIGHT

These royal portrayals of the swan, however, do not quite
account for the astonishingly widespread usage of the
swan as an emblem within European courts. The rise in the
swan's popularity began with Godfrey of Bouillon, a leader
of the First Crusade and ruler of Jerusalem (r. 1099–1100).[7]
While early chronicles list Godfrey as one of several men
instrumental in the Crusades' success, later accounts,
such as *Historia Ierosolimitana* (c.1125–50), place Godfrey
as the central figure.[8] Godfrey's success in the First

Crusade circulated around the same time as early Swan Knight tales, and the two became fused. As Crusade stories increased in popularity, Godfrey and his brothers became explicitly named as the descendants of the legendary Swan Knight.

By 1170 Guy of Bazoches identifies Baldwin, Godfrey's brother, with the Swan Knight: 'Nepos militis ejus, per vada cui Rheni dux fuit albus olor' (He is the grandson of that knight, to whom the white swan was guide through the shallows of the Rhine).[9] Others, such as Geoffrey of Clairvaux (1187–8) and Hélinand of Froidmont (1211–23), mention the knight drawn by a swan, or 'miles cigni'.[10] William of Tyre, in his influential account of the Crusades (c.1170), discredits rumours that link Godfrey to the Swan Knight:

> Preterimus denique studiose, licet id verum fuisse plurimorum astruat narratio, cigni fabulam, unde vulgo dicitur sementivam eis fuisse originem, eo quod a vero videatur deficere talis assertion.

> I purposely omit the story of the swan whence, legend declares, these brothers derived their origin, because, although many writers give that as true, yet it seems to be without foundation.[11]

The fictitious histories of the First Crusade in the Old French Crusade Cycle promoted the Swan Knight as Godfrey's ancestor. The *Chanson d'Antioche* (c.1180s) tells us: 'Son avie a duist uns cisnes a Nimaeie el sablon [...] Une fille en remest el castel de Bullon, / Li dus Godefrois est de cele estracion' (His ancestor was brought by a swan to the sandy riverbanks at Nijmegen. [...] A daughter was left behind in the castle of Bouillon; and Duke Godfrey is descended from her).[12]

The next sequence in the Crusade Cycle, *La Chanson de Jérusalem*, identifies Godfrey as the Swan Knight's grandson: 'Qui sa mere engenra / Li Chevaliers au chisne' (The one whose mother was fathered by the Swan Knight).[13] Later, his brother Eustace compares Godfrey to their legendary ancestor: 'Frere, or vos ai véu: / De ces grans cops sanblés nostre aiol qui ja fu, / Le chevalier au chisne' (Brother, I have seen well how your mighty blows make you look like our ancestor, the Swan Knight).[14]

The Old French Crusade Cycle solidifies the link between Godfrey and the Swan Knight through *La Naissance, Le Chevalier au Cygne, La Fin d'Elias, Les Enfances Godefroi*, and *Le Retour de Cornumarant*.[15] These texts relay the entire story of the Swan Knight: from his birth as septuplet, to his swan transformation, to his knightly exploits with his swan-sibling, to his marriage, and importantly, his progeny, which focuses on Godfrey.

Soon Godfrey became one of the great medieval heroes, taking his place besides Charlemagne and King Arthur as one of the Nine Worthies. Images of the Nine Worthies circulated widely throughout Europe – on tapestries, illuminations, and stone reliefs decorating chapels, buildings, and fountains (Figure 8). Between Godfrey's fame in the First Crusade, his Swan Knight ancestry, and his seat among the Nine Worthies, perhaps it comes as no surprise that houses throughout Europe competed to be associated with his dynastic lineage.[16]

GERMANIC AND DUTCH ASSOCIATIONS WITH
THE SWAN KNIGHT

Swan Knight ancestry shaped identities, geographies, and histories in medieval German and Dutch households. Many noble families commissioned works to prove their dynastic connection to the Swan Knight. Families who laid particular claim as his descendants were the houses of Brabant, Cleves, and Brandenburg.[17] Wolfram von Eschenbach's Lohengrin rescues the mistress of Brabant, aligning the Swan Knight with the Duchy of Brabant and the Holy Roman Empire.[18] Konrad von Würzburg's *Schwanritter* has the Swan Knight rescuing the Duke of Brabant's widow, and from them descend the houses of Cleves, Guelders, and Rheinecks.

Figure 8: *The Nine Worthies, thirteenth century. Cologne, Cologne City Hall. © Raimond Spekking / CC BY-SA 4.0. The three Christian Worthies appear on the far left: Charlemagne with an eagle on his shield; King Arthur with a shield of three crowns; and Godfrey of Bouillon, with a little dog at his feet and sword and shield in his hands.*

Von Gelre beidiu und von Clëven die grâven sint von in bekomen und wurden Rienecker genomen ûჳ ir geslehte vërre erkant.

The counts of both Guelders and Cleves are descended from them, and the counts of Rienecker are descended from their widely recognised family.[19]

For the line of Cleves, this ancestry was particularly celebrated.[20] Their ancestral home is Schwanenburg (Swan Castle) (c.1020), located along the Northern Rhine. Legend has it that Beatrice of Cleves married the Swan Knight, and after his departure, she lived in 'Schwanenturm' (Swan Tower) until her death. The Chronicles of the Dukes of Clèves (fifteenth century) depict Beatrice of Cleves in her Swan Tower receiving the Swan Knight (Plate 5).

Later generations of Cleves celebrated their ancestry through courtly displays. On 17 February 1454, Adolph of Cleves, Lord of Ravenstein (1425–92), pretended to be the Swan Knight at a sumptuous Feast of the Pheasant held by his uncle, Philip the Good, Duke of Burgundy. The festivities opened with a joust, where it was announced that the Swan Knight would compete and the joust's winner would receive a bejewelled swan of gold, chained with a golden chain, and at the end of the chain was a ruby.[21] The Swan Knight was also a principal theme at the feast. On the banquet table stood a ship drawn by a silver swan with a golden chain, and in the boat was a knight wearing the arms of the house of Cleves. An eyewitness, Olivier de la Marche relays its significance:

> Et me fut dit que ce signiffioit et monstroit, comme jadiz miraculeusement ung signe amena dedans une nef, par la riviere du Rin, ung chevalier au chasteau de Cleves, lequel fut moult vertueulx et vaillant, et l'epousa la princesse du pays, qui pour lors estoit vefve et en eut lignée, dont lesditz ducs de Cleves, jusques à ce jour, sont yssuz.

And I was told that this represented how miraculously
of old a swan brought in a ship by the river Rhine to the
castle of Cleves a very virtuous and valiant knight who
married the princess of the country and by her had issue
from whom sprung the dukes of Cleves even to this day.[22]

The joust of the Swan Knight, the swan jewel, and the Swan
Knight in banquet décor thoroughly showcase the Cleves'
illustrious lineage. Years later, Marie de Cleves (d. 1487),
the widow of Charles d'Orleans (d. 1465), commissioned an
abridged Crusade Cycle, intended in the words of Simon
John to 'cement the dynastic connection between the Swan
Knight and the house of Cleves'.[23]

The house of Brabant competed with the house of
Cleves for Swan Knight ancestry. Jacob of Maerlant's Middle
Dutch *Spiegel Historiael* (thirteenth century) has the dukes
of Brabant as Swan Knight descendants.[24] Wolfram von
Eschenbach's Lohengrin rescues the princess of Brabant. In
the medieval *Lohengrin* the Swan Knight rescues Elsam of
Brabant and their descendants form the houses of Brabant,
Guelders, and Cleves. The narrative was likely written to
heighten their familial connection to the Swan Knight.
Lorengel also concludes with the hero ruling Brabant.

The house of Brandenburg also claimed Swan Knight
ancestry. The arms of Florian Waldauff feature the Swan of
Brandenburg (*c*.1520).[25] With the rise of chivalric orders,
such as the Order of the Garter (1348), came the Order of
the Swan (*c*.1440). Also known as the 'Society of Our Lady',
the Order of the Swan was established by Friedrich II von
Hohenzollern, Elector-Marquis of Brandenburg.[26] Religious
in nature, the order held the chapel of the Order of the Swan
in Ansbach.[27] Members wore an elaborate collar, decorated

with hearts and instruments of torture, with two pendants: one of the Virgin and one of a swan.[28] They swore to love one another and report libel.[29] Another swan order also existed. In 1350, at the marriage festivities of his sister, Count Amé [Amédée] VI of Savoy created the 'Companie du Cigne Noir' (Company of the Black Swan). Although short-lived, this was a fraternal order, a band of 'brothers-in-arms' or allies, bound to aid each other in military enterprise.[30]

The swan featured in medieval German heraldry, tomb-etchings (Figure 9), and topography. An entire region of Bavaria is called 'Schwangao' (Swan region),which has three castles associated with swans. The first is Schloss Hohenschwangau (twelfth century), home to the Counts of Schwangau, including the minstrel Hiltbolt von Schwangau (1195–1254).[31] Black swans adorn his attire (Plate 6). Schloss Hohenschwangau was later acquired by the Bavarian royal family and used as the summer residence of King Maximilian II. The other two swan castles – Vorderhohenschwangau and Hinterhohenschwangau – were eventually reconstructed by King Ludwig II into Neuschwanstein – New Swan Castle.

THE SWAN KNIGHT AND FRANCE

The French have perhaps the most direct claim to Swan Knight ancestry. While Godfrey of Bouillon died in Jerusalem, his brother Eustace returned home, took up the dukedom of Bouillon, and married. His descendants, the Counts of Bouillon and Ardennes, had a direct claim to Swan Knight heritage. Their lineage is made explicit in the Old French Crusade Cycle text *Les Enfances Godefroi*. French

Figure 9: *Tomb of Rudolf von Sachsenhausen (d. 1371). Frankfurt, Frankfurt Cathedral. Photograph: Marcel Schawe © Dommuseum Frankfurt. The swan appears on Rudolf's headdress and twice on his shield, emphasising the swan as his heraldic emblem.*

royals were also Swan Knight descendants, including King John II (d. 1364) and his two sons – King Charles V (d. 1380) and John, Duke of Berry (d. 1416). John had a double claim to Swan Knight lineage through his wife Jeanne, Countess of Auvergne and Bouillon (d. 1422) – also an alleged Swan Knight descendant. Swans became one of John's personal emblems. Swans permeate his commissioned manuscript, the *Très Riches Heures*, seen on maizers, tapestries, and in moats. Cazelles and Rathofer hypothesise about the swan's significance for John:

> The swan, usually with a bloodstained wound in its breast, derives from the period around 1364 when Jean de Berry was held hostage in England. He became [...] enamored of a 'dame anglaische servante au Dieu d'amours' ('an English lady in the service of the god of love') for whom he placed beneath his shield 'le cygne blanc navré' ('the wounded white swan').[32]

For John, the swan appears to symbolise courtly love.

The dukes of Burgundy also claimed descent from the Swan Knight. D'Hulst writes: 'The legendary Swan Knight was a hero loved and venerated at the court, since he was recognised as a forefather of the House of Burgundy.'[33] A patron of the arts, Philip the Bold (1342–1404) commissioned a tapestry featuring Godfrey of Bouillon, owned the sword of Godfrey (acquired 13 March 1393), and adorned his clothing with swans.[34]

His grandson Philip the Good (1396–1467) also appreciated swan splendour. In 1462 he bought *The Knight of the Swan* tapestry produced by Pasquier Grenier (d. 1493), tapestry weaver and merchant.[35] Philip's other tapestries featured Godfrey of Bouillon.[36] At Philip's Feast of the Pheasant, the Swan Knight jousted and featured in table décor. Philip was a close ally of Henry V, who also claimed Swan Knight ancestry and adopted the swan as a crest.[37] Philip also inherited the Brabant lands – which too had known Swan Knight affiliations.[38]

SWAN KNIGHT ANCESTRY AND ENGLISH POLITICS

Matilda and Stephen

Swan Knight Ancestry was linked, very early, to the English throne. It began in 1125 with the marriage of King Stephen of Blois (d. 1154) to Matilda (d. 1152), the daughter of Eustace of Bouillon, Godfrey's brother (d. 1100). Matilda and Stephen founded Faversham Abbey in 1148. Its library held a copy of The Red Book of the Exchequer (Liber Rubeus de Scaccario) – a book that pronounced their Swan Knight lineage. It tells of the swan with the golden chain, and proceeds to name the Swan Knight's descendants: Godfrey, Baldwin, and 'Eustachio Magno' 'de qua genuit Matilldem postmodum Reginam Anglorum' (Eustace the Great, who begat Matilda, afterwards Queen of England).[39] Their progeny married into the houses of Dammartin, Bohun, Warwick, Tony, Stafford, and the royal house of Lancaster.[40] Their early descendants included Ferdinand III, King of Castile (d. 1252) and Edward I, King of England (d. 1307).

Edward I

Probably to celebrate his Swan Knight lineage, Edward I prominently featured the swan during his reign. One significant occasion was the splendid Feast of the Swan. In need of more knights to face Robert the Bruce in Scotland, Edward remedied his shortage of knights by creating them. He held a mass knighting ceremony on 22 May 1306.[41] At the ceremony, Edward knighted his son, the future Edward II. The prince in turn knighted over three hundred men. During the feast that followed, Edward made vows before two swans dressed in gold. The account of *Flores Historiarum* reads:

> Tunc allati sunt in pompatica gloria duo cigni vel olores ante regem, phalerati retibus aureis vel fistulis deauratis, desiderabile spectaculum intuentibus. Quibus visis, rex vovit votum Deo caeli et cignis se velle proficisci in Scotiam, sanctae Ecclesiae injuriam ac mortem Johannis Comyn et fidem laesam Scotorum vindicaturus, mortuus sive vivus. Sponderent igitur illud votum caeteri magnates fide bona asserentes se secum paratos esse in vita regis et post mortem ipsius cum filio suo principe in Scotiam proficisci, votum regium expleturos.

> Then two cygnets or swans, ornamented with golden nets or gilded pipings, were brought in in showy splendour before the king; an agreeable spectacle to those looking on. Having looked at them, the king vowed a vow to God in heaven and the cygnets (or swans) that he purposed to set out for Scotland, to avenge the injury done to Holy Church, the death of John Comyn and the broken faith of the Scots, dead or alive. Thereupon the other nobles bound themselves by the same oath,

affirming in good faith that they were prepared to set out for Scotland with the king while he lived and, after his death, with the Prince, his son, in order to fulfil the royal vow.[42]

Why the swan was specifically chosen to witness this vow is uncertain, but it appears to have established a precedent of knights swearing binding oaths upon birds, such as herons, pheasants, peacocks, or other noble birds.[43] Philip the Good's Feast of the Pheasant at Lille in 1454 is one example.

The Bohuns

During the knighting ceremony that preceded the Feast of the Swan, one gilt spur was fastened onto the Crown Prince by his brother-in-law, Humphrey de Bohun (d. 1321). Claiming Swan Knight ancestry from Stephen and Matilda, Humphrey married into the royal family when he wed Edward I's daughter, Elizabeth (d. 1328). Humphrey made much of his ancestry. He was one of the first to use the swan as badge, seen in the Counter Seal attached to the Barons' Letter of 1301 (Figure 10).[44] His will of 1319 bequeathed to his son bed furnishings of green spotted with swans.[45] In a list of goods that were seized from Humphrey in 1322 were clerical items – an alb and stole embroidered with swans and leopards.[46] Amongst his goods held at Walden Abbey were eighteen green bench-covers and tapestries with swans.[47] Celebrating his swan lineage, he named his sixth son Aeneas, the name of the Swan Knight in Middle English (Enyas).[48] He likely commissioned the amazing Bohun saddle device, where a

Figure 10: *Seal of Humphrey de Bohun appended to Barons' Letter 1301. Kew, the National Archives, E26. Engraving by George Vertue in 1729 based on facsimile of Augustine Vincent's manuscript of 1624. Public domain. Humphrey de Bohun (d. 1321) proudly celebrated his Swan Knight lineage and was one of the first to use the swan as his personal seal.*

swan sits at the base of the pommel.[49] In Pleshey Castle, the Bohun residence, hung tapestries of Godfrey of Bouillon and their library held a copy of Godfrey's history.[50] As the swan grew to be associated with the Bohuns, it featured on their crest.

Humphrey and Elizabeth's daughter Margaret de Bohun (d. 1391) married Hugh of Courtenay, Earl of Devon (d. 1377). Her swan-ancestry is celebrated in a resplendent effigy over her tomb in Exeter Cathedral of two mourning swans (Figure 11). Margaret's grandson, Peter Courtney was Bishop of Exeter Cathedral (1478–87). His coat of arms stands over the mantelpiece in the Bishop's Palace in Exeter Cathedral, featuring two swans collared by a golden chain (Plate 7). This chained and collared swan became known as the Bohun Swan. The Sherborne Missal features the Bohun Swan, described as 'a swan proper, a gold crown and chain about the neck' (Figure 12).[51]

Edward III

Associated with his father and grandfather, swans were also employed by Edward III (d. 1377). In a list of items for Edward's Christmas Games (1347) is a reference to fourteen

Figure 11: *Ducally gorged Bohun swans on tomb of Margaret de Bohun (1311–91). Exeter, Exeter Cathedral. Public domain. The swans with a collar and chain, a feature also referred to as 'ducally gorged', became known as 'Bohun swans'. The collar and chain likely refer to Swan Knight stories, where the swan uses a chain to pull the knight in a boat.*

Figure 12: *The Bohun Swan*, *c.*1399–1407. *London, British Library, Sherborne Missal*, Add. *MS* 74236, *p.* 365 *col. i.*
© *British Library Board.*

swans' heads and fourteen pairs of wings.[52] Presumably these were used for festive costume or fancy dress parties. A swan also featured in Edward III's motto. His motto appears in a list of items gathered for the Christmas Games of 1348, listed by Vale:

> 1 complete buckram harness [i.e. armour for man and horse] for the king, spangled with silver, the tunic and shield worked with the king's motto, 'Hay hay the wythe swan by goddes soule I am thy man'.[53]

The 'wythe swan' may be Edward himself. Or it may be the bird that witnesses his vow to be 'thy man'. His son Edward the Black Prince in his will issued worsted wall hangings with swans and mermaids to his son – the future Richard II.[54] As illustrated from Edward I to the Black Prince, swans consistently recur as an emblem of the English monarchs.

Swans Badges and Richard II

As the swan was a symbol of Richard II's forefathers, Richard's own treasury contained many jewelled swans, some bearing royal arms.[55] But during Richard's reign, the swan developed into a political symbol that threatened his rule. Crowned at ten, Richard II was initially governed by his uncles, John of Gaunt, Duke of Lancaster ('Lancaster') (d. 1399) and Thomas of Woodstock, Duke of Gloucester (known as 'Woodstock' or 'Gloucester') (d. 1397) – both sons of Edward III. The swan was Woodstock's emblem, thanks to his marriage to Eleanor de Bohun (d. 1399), and featured in his seal and badge (Plate 8).[56] In her will, Eleanor bequeathed a book of swan romances to their son Humphrey; a swan is etched on her tomb in Westminster Abbey.[57] Eleanor's sister Mary de Bohun (d. 1349) married Henry Bolingbroke (d. 1413), the son of John of Gaunt, who also adopted the swan as his symbol.

Woodstock and Bolingbroke joined a group of nobles who opposed the tight nucleus of power that surrounded Richard II. Known as the Lords Appellant, this cadre defeated the armies of the king's favourites. In the Merciless Parliament of 1388, the Lords Appellant sentenced eight of Richard's advisors to execution, others to exile.[58] Ten years later, Richard had his revenge. He exiled Bolingbroke and personally arrested his uncle Woodstock, who was murdered whilst awaiting trial.

Woodstock's arrest saw his possessions forfeited to the crown. Many of them are recorded in Richard II's Treasury Rolls. Woodstock's items include: a signet ring with a swan; a mitre with two interlacing swan necks; and a salt cellar shaped as a swan.[59] Other swans appear in the Treasury

Roll, also likely Woodstock's – a swan brooch and a candelabra with a pair of Bohun swans.[60] These swans emphasise the extent to which Woodstock rooted his identity in his Swan Knight ancestry.

Perhaps the most beautiful item of Woodstock's listed in Richard II's treasury is a swan pendant. The Roll reads:

> **R 488** Item, j cigne d'or aimell' blanc ove j petit cheine d'or pendant entour le cool, pois' ij unc', priz xlvjs. viijd.

> Item, a gold swan enamelled white with a little gold chain hanging around the neck, weighing 2 oz., value, 46s. 8d.[61]

This description evokes the joust prize at the Feast of the Pheasant – both jewelled swans, ducally gorged. While R488 is unrecovered, its description is similar to the extant Dunstable Jewel. Made of delicate, white enamel, the Dunstable swan, only one inch square, was worn on clothing as a badge (Plate 9).[62]

These swans may have been gifts from the French Court. Like Bolingbroke and Woodstock, John Duke of Berry adopted the swan as his badge. Gifts were exchanged between Berry, Lancaster, and Woodstock in the wedding negotiations between Richard II and Isabella of Valois (1389–1409).[63] Perhaps it is due to this shared emblem between Berry, Woodstock, and Bolingbroke that costly swans appear in the English Royal Treasury.

Livery Badges
Both swans – Woodstock's pendant and the Dunstable Jewel – were likely livery badges. A livery badge was an item worn on clothing (such as the chest, sleeve or neck) that

symbolised support for their distributor.[64] As nobles vied with Richard II for power, the distribution of badges created private armies, curried favour with recruits, and denoted support either for or against the king.[65] The swan appears to have been distributed as a livery badge to support

Figure 13: *Flag of Buckinghamshire, background of red and white, with ducally gorged swan. Image: Graham Bartram. Public domain. Compare to Plate 8. Black and red were the colours of Thomas of Woodstock and the ducally gorged swan was his personal emblem. Woodstock's livery was inherited by the dukes of Buckingham, reflected today in the arms and flags of Buckinghamshire.*

Woodstock and Bolingbroke. In 1393 Bolingbroke gave a livery collar to the poet John Gower.[66] The collar was unique to Bolingbroke. It consisted of a collar of Esses, inherited from his father, with a swan pendant at its base, a mark of his marriage into the Bohun family. The collar is depicted on Gower's tomb effigy in Southwark Cathedral.[67] The swan collar Bolingbroke gifted Gower, or the swan pendant seized by Richard II, or other surviving swan badges held in the British Museum, indicate the extent to which swans were distributed as a political item, likely denoting support for Bolingbroke and Woodstock.[68]

Before long livery badges began to cause political upheaval. One of John of Gaunt's knights was mobbed for wearing Gaunt's livery collar.[69] The House of Commons, and even Richard II, recommended abandoning badges, but the Lords were unwilling to relinquish the badges' power. New laws in 1390 restricted the use of badges, which were now 'only to be worn as part of a formal and properly consti-tuted life contract', writes Given-Wilson.[70] Richard II began to issue his badge of the White Hart – collared with a golden crown around its neck – likely given to unruly nobles to secure their submission (Plate 10). The first recorded instance was in October 1390 at the Smithfield tournament: 'Ubi datum erat primo signum vel stigma illud egregium in cervo albo, cum corona et cathena aurea' (Where first was given that excellent sign or badge in [the form of] a white hart, with a golden crown and chain).[71] Retrospectively, the supporters of Richard II were described as those 'that had hertis / on hie on her brestis'.[72] Richard's White Hart is nearly a perfect foil to the White Bohun Swan: both are white animals tethered about the neck with a golden crown and chain (Plates 9 and 10). Their similarities, perhaps, further emphasise the swan as a symbol of Richard's rivals, used to undermine Richard's rule. By the century's end a new law passed allowing only the king to distribute badges and to no one below the rank of esquire.[73] Richard, however, continued to seize the lands and goods of his nobles. It was Richard's behaviour to his uncles – the murder of Woodstock and the seizure of John of Gaunt's bequeathed estate – that escalated conflict. Seen as capricious and unstable, Richard II was deposed in 1399, succeeded by Henry Bolingbroke – Henry IV.[74]

The House of Lancaster
With Henry IV's ascent to the throne, the symbol of the swan won out over the hart. Poems quickly circulated that denounced the murder of Woodstock, highlighted Richard II's inadequacy, and defended Henry IV's authority and rule. Two poems describe those murdered by Richard through their heraldic devices. Twice Woodstock is referred to as 'the swan': 'Thorw the busch a swan was sclayn' and later 'The swan is ded'.[75] The gloss identifies the swan as the Duke of Gloucester, Thomas of Woodstock. Gower justified Bolingbroke's usurpation in *Cronica tripertita*.[76] Woodstock he called 'Cignus benignus' (the gentle swan) and calls for the vindication of justice at his death.[77]

With Henry's coronation, the swan become the symbol of the new king. The Sherborne Missal depicts the coat of arms of Henry IV, with a white swan holding a scroll that reads 'Rex Anglie' (Figure 14). He incorporated the swan into his livery badge. Swans adorn his tomb and the tomb of his wife, Mary de Bohun.[78]

Figure 14: *Arms of Henry IV and swan, 1399–1407. London, British Library, Sherborne Missal, Add. MS 74236 Missal, p. 80 col. i. © British Library Board. The swan surrounds Henry's coat of arms and the script in its bill reads 'Rex Anglie'.*

The swan was also a symbol of his son, Henry V. The swan was incorporated into Henry V's coat of arms. In the Sherborne Missal, a swan stands next to his coat of arms, with a scroll that reads 'Prynceps Wallie' (Figure 15).[79] Swans also adorned Henry V's livery, promoted by his father. Ward states that in 1401 Henry IV's son 'Prince Henry was permitted to use a swan pendant on his SS collars'.[80] Swans decorated his coronation banquet and adorned his tomb.[81]

Passed down, the swan was a personal emblem of Henry VI – the son of Henry V and Margaret of Anjou. During Henry VI's unstable reign, the swan was used as livery badge to quell unrest. Cherry writes, 'in 1459 Margaret made him [Henry VI] give out the livery of swans to all the gentlemen of Cheshire in order to quash rumours that he was not her child'.[82] Although Henry VI was later deposed, his swan symbol became an emblem around which forces rallied

Figure 15: *Arms of Henry Prince of Wales (the future Henry V),
1399–1407. London, British Library, Sherborne Missal, Add.
MS 74236, p. 81 col. ii. © British Library Board. The swan was
also a symbol of the future Henry V. The swan's scroll reads 'Prynceps
Wallie' (Prince of Wales).*

in the War of the Roses. The swan developed into an
important emblem, not just for Henry IV, but for the House
of Lancaster.

The Wars of the Roses
The deposition of Henry VI precipitated the Wars of the
Roses between the houses of York and Lancaster. During
this period, the swan symbolised not only the Lancasters,
but two of the most powerful men in the realm – the Earl of
Warwick and the Duke of Buckingham.

The house of Warwick claimed Swan Knight ancestry
through the Beauchamps and the Tonys.[83] Their descent
from the Swan Knight is made explicit in the Rous Roll
(c.1484). John Rous' roll contains a short history of the
swan children, who 'were forshapyd un to swannys with

colers and chenys of gold'.[84] The swan with golden collar and chain evokes the Dunstable Jewel depiction – the Bohun and Lancastrian swan (Plate 9). It is likely the stories of swan children inspired the badge's depiction. John Rous clarifies the link between the Earls of Warwick and Enyas (Eneas) – the Middle English name for the Swan Knight, 'of wyche sir Eneas descendid many grete lords and ladies and speciall the Eorlis of Warwik'.[85] The proof of ancestry John supplies: 'In whos tresori was kept ye cup made of the cheyn a for seyd I have dronk of the same'.[86] For Rous, Warwick's lineage is proven by his possession of a family heirloom— the goblet made from one of the swan's golden chains, an integral component to the Swan Knight legends.

The Dukes of Buckingham inherited Woodstock's livery – the swan argent against black and red. The shield was later adopted as town arms of Buckingham (Figure 13). In the sixteenth century, Robert Copland translated a concise trilogy of the Swan Knight – from swan septuplets to Godfrey's exploits in Jerusalem – at the bequest of Edward Stafford (d. 1521), Duke of Buckingham, Earl of Hereford, Stafford and Northampton. Its purpose was to prove descent between the Swan Knight and Buckingham: 'Helyas the Knight of the swanne of whom linially is dyscended my sayde Lorde', writes Copland.[87]

In the Wars of the Roses, both the Earl of Warwick and the Duke of Buckingham opposed the house of Plantagenet. England's most powerful noble, Richard de Neville, 16th Earl of Warwick (d. 1471) rebelled in 1469. He withdrew his support from Edward IV and sided with the Lancastrians and Henry VI.[88] In 1483, Henry Stafford, 2nd Duke of

Buckingham, instigated a rebellion against the usurper Richard III. Buckingham's rebellion began to prompt forces to promote Henry Tudor – the future Henry VII – to the throne.[89] But the swan was not a symbol of the house of Tudor. During the Tudor Age in England, the swan became a commodity increasingly controlled by the Crown. Dining on swans, and the hefty cost of doing so, caused swan husbandry and ownership to be contested and then controlled by English monarchs, eventually causing all unmarked swans to become property of the Crown.

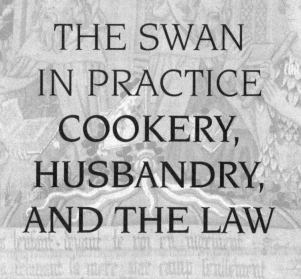

THE SWAN
IN PRACTICE
COOKERY,
HUSBANDRY,
AND THE LAW

APART FROM being allegorical, literary, or political figures, swans were physical creatures that inhabited medieval Europe. People reared swans, cooked swans, dined on swans, and fought legal battles over the ownership of swans. Swan ownership was frequently disputed because swans were costly and impressive banquet dishes. In England, this eventually led to swans becoming almost solely the property of the Crown. To analyse the swan's transition from semi-feral bird to regal property, the final third of this chapter will examine evidence beyond the Middle Ages.

THE SWAN AT FEASTS

Cooked swan was a delicacy served at medieval feasts and banquets. On special occasions, swans were consumed in large numbers. In 1251, Henry III (1207–72) ordered over 125 swans for his Christmas Day feast at York.[1] Over twenty pairs of cygnets were ordered in 1504 for the Bishop of Durham's Christmas Feast.[2] When George Neville became Archbishop of York in 1466, the celebration feast served over 400 swans.[3] Swans were often kept in nearby regions (often termed 'boroughs') and were summoned for feast days. For example, the Durham Priory Manorial Accounts

(1277–1306) record that three swans were sent for the feast of St. Cuthbert, Durham's patron saint, nearly a tenth of the flock.[4] The Crown could levy swans from neighbouring boroughs. For Henry III's Christmas feast, York supplied 'xxx cingnis' (30 swans), while Northumberland, Lancaster, and Cumberland each supplied 'xv cignis' (15 swans).[5]

Swans were one of many dishes served at elaborate feasts. In Edward I's famous Feast of the Swan (1306), swans were one part of a sumptuous display. The Close Rolls record the arrivals of dozens of peacocks, swans, hares, pheasants, a thousand chickens, and two thousand eggs.[6] The sumptuousness of the Swan Feast is evident when compared to a typical luxurious feast for Easter or Whitsun, where a local region might be required to produce six swans, six peacocks, a hundred hares, and two boars.[7] Swans appear in an Anglo-Norman menu in the 'Treatise of Walter of Bibbesworth' (thirteenth century), which included cranes, peacocks, swans, kids (young goats), pigs, hens, rabbits in gravy, pheasants, woodcocks, partridges, thrushes, larks, plovers, blackbirds, crêpes, candied mace, and wafers.[8] In France, swans were served in the second course; in England, the first. John Russell's *Boke of Nurture* (*c.*1440–50) includes swan with chawdron in the first course, alongside boiled beef, mutton, pheasant, baked venison, and capon.[9]

HOW TO COOK A SWAN IN FRANCE

In France swans featured in feasts as opulent marvels. One example occurs in Master Chiquart's *Du fait de cuisine* (1420). In it, he explains how to construct castles of pastry – so large that it took four persons to carry them on a litter.

Decorated with archers and crossbowmen, the castle had four towers: in the first, a boar's head; in the second, a pike; in the third, a glazed piglet, and in the fourth 'au pie de lautre tour ung cigne escorchies / et revetuz aussi gectant feu' (at the foot of the last tower a skinned and redressed swan, likewise breathing fire).[10] Master Chiquart gives detailed instructions to make these animals breath fire:

> Pour faire quelles donnent ꝗ lancent feu par la gorge si prennes / 25v/ ung doublet de cire · et si lenveloppes tout denviron de coton qui soit moilliez en eaue ardant fine ꝗ pure dun pou de canfre.

> To make them give out and breathe fire by their mouths, take /25v/ a double-wicked wax candle and wrap it around with cotton which has been moistened in firewater in which a little camphor has been dissolved.[11]

Fire-breathing creatures combined food with spectacle. Scully comments on this process: 'By soaking cotton in *aqua ardens* and igniting it at the right moment, the animal could continue for some time to do the impossible while it was paraded on a platter around the dining hall.'[12] Pastry castles with fire breathing animals included the swan in displays the combined dining with spectacle.

Redressing a cooked swan was another aspect of marvellous dining displays.[13] The purpose of redressing a cooked swan was to make it appear as life-like as possible. To redress a swan, its skin had to be kept carefully intact. By inserting a straw between the skin and flesh, and inflating the space in between, the cook separated the skin from the flesh in one piece. The carcass was then removed and roasted, and then 'redressed', or inserted back into its own skin and feathers. The redressed swan was served cooked but appeared alive. Sometimes it was served with its neck erect, thanks to careful stengthening, and its wings outstretched.[14] The marvel of a cooked swan, resplendent with feathers, its wings outstretched (some two meters), and breathing fire, as a meal to then partake and consume – lifelike and yet lifeless – would surely have astonished its audience.

The effect of surprise is a prominent theme in medieval cookery texts. While the redressed swan was cooked but appeared alive, the reverse was also practiced. Cruel for the bird, the directions in the fifteenth-century *Vivendier* instruct that any fowl (swans seemingly included) be taken, plucked alive, painted in a golden *jus* to appear cooked, and then served. *The Vivendier* reads: 'Quant on le vaura trenchier il se esveillera et s'en fuira par la table at abatra pos et hanaps, etc.' (When it is about to be carved it will wake up and make off down the table upsetting jugs, goblets and whatnot).[15] The effect of this surprise is conditional upon the bird looking cooked or golden. Roasted swans were frequently basted in a 'golden jus' to achieve this colour – called 'dorer'. The sauce was made of yellow colours – eggs, saffron, and breadcrumbs soaked in wine.[16] The neck and head were reserved for eminent persons, the rest served to others.[17]

HOW TO COOK A SWAN IN ENGLAND

In England, the swan appeared in a spectacle that combined dining and politics. Because swans were the personal emblem of Henry V, his coronation feast featured swans in pageant display. The cookery account gives instructions to present: 'A gret swan for suttellte sittinge upon a grene stok displaid with a skriptur in his bille / *Regardez Roy la droyt voy* (A great swan for subtlety, sitting upon a green base displayed with a scroll in his bill / *King, behold the right way*).[18] This was to be followed by six cygnets each with a different portion of this writing in its bill: *Theney la ley / Gardez la fey / Hors de court Soit bannez tort / Eyez pete des comunalte* (Keep the law / Protect the faith / Let wrong be banished from the court / Have pity on the poor). This dish was succeeded by a procession of 'xxiiij swannys euychon of them a byll in the mouthe, / *noble honour and joy*' (twenty-four swans each one of them with a bill in its mouth reading *noble honour and joy*). Swans also decorated jellies in the second course.

Swans were a banqueting delicacy, frequently spitted and roasted. The fourteenth-century English recipe book *Curye on Inglysch* provides these instructions.

> 11. For to dihȝte a swan. Tak & vndo hym & wasch hym, & do on a spite & enarme hym fayre & roste hym wel; & dysmembre hym on þe beste manere & mak a fayre chyne, & þe sauce þerto schal be mad in þis manere, & it is clept: chauden'.[19]

> For the preparation of a swan. Take and undo him and wash him and put him on a spit and garnish him fair and roast him well; and dismember him in the best manner and make a fair cut of meat and the sauce thereto shall be made in this manner and it is called: chauden.

In England, swans were frequently paired with 'chawdoun sauce'. A recipe for this sauce, made from the offal of swans, is provided by the 'chef Maister Cokes of kyng Richard the Se|cu|nde kyng of |En|glond':

> 147 Chawdoun for swannes. Take þe lyuer and þe offall of the swannes, & do it to seeþ in gode broth; take it vp. Pyke out þe bonys; take & hewe the flessh smale. Make a lyour of crustes of brede & of þe blode of þe swan ysoden, & do þerto powdour of gynger, of clowes, & of piper, & a litul wyne & salt, & seeþ it, & cast þe flessh þerto ihewed; & messe it forth with þe swan irostede.[20]

> Chawdoun of swans. Take the liver and the offal of the swans and seethe it in good broth. Take it up. Pick out the bones. Take and hew the flesh small. Make a layer of crusts of bread and of the blood of the same swan and add powdered ginger, cloves, pepper, and a little wine and salt, and seethe it. And cast the flesh hewed into it. And serve it with the roasted swan.

Chawdoun of swans was an especially English dish. Others included boiled swans' feet.[21]

OLIM LACUS

Feasting on swans obviously meant their death. The connection between the swan's death and its role as banquet entrée brought to the mind of one twelfth-century cleric the swan's fabled death-song. The swan's death-song is given a new twist in the *Carmina Burana*, a twelfth-century collection of bawdy and humorous Latin verses. In *Olim lacus*, the swan sings about its own death for the purpose of garnishing the banquet table:

1. Olim lacus colueram,   1. Once I had lakes to live upon:
olim pulcher extiteram,   in glory I would swim along –
dum cignus ego fueram.   once, when I was still a swan.
    miser, miser!   Misery, Misery!
Refl. Modo niger   Now black
    et ustus fortiter.   And well roasted.

2. Girat, regirat carcifer,   Cook on the spit is turning me,
propinat me nunc dapifer,   flames sear through every nerve
                     in me –
me rogus urit fortiter.   now here's a waitor serving me!
    miser, miser!   Misery, Misery!
<Refl. Modo niger …>   <Refrain: Now black …>

3. Mallem in aquis uiuere,   I'd rather be in the fresh air
nudo semper sub aere,   out on a lake – or anywhere
quam in hoc mergi pipere.   but peppered up as
                    gourmet's fare.
    miser, miser!   Misery, Misery!
<Refl. Modo niger …>   <Refrain: Now black …>

4. Eram niue candidior,   Once I was whiter than snow,
quauis aue formosior,   finer than any bird I know:
modo sum coruo nigrior.   now see me – blacker than a crow!
    miser, miser!   Misery, Misery!
<Refl. Modo niger …>   <Refrain: Now black …>

5. Nunc in scutella iaceo	Here in this serving dish I lie
et uolitare nequeo,	where I have no strength to fly
dentes frendentes uideo –	as grinding molars greet the eye –
miser, miser!	Misery, Misery!
<Refl. Modo niger ...>	<Refrain: Now black ...>[22]

With its pronounced rhyme and rhythm, unusual to classical verse, this song provides a humorous rendition of the death-song the swan might sing as it was being served. It is noticeably a lament, with its repetition of 'miser, miser', reiterating the trope that swans mourn their death. As in *Clangam, filii*, the human voice supplies the swan's song.

THE VALUE OF SWANS

Due to its prominence at feasts, the swan was a fowl of great worth. It was the most expensive fowl in medieval accounts. In the *Statura Poletriae* of London City in 1274, a swan sold for three shillings, a goose for five pence, a pheasant for four pence.[23] One could buy seven geese for the price of one swan. Although the price of swans was fixed at three shillings from roughly 1274–1415, private household records show that swans often sold for much more – up to six shillings and eight pence – more than twice the London price.

Because of their worth, swans made costly gifts. In 1475, Edward IV gave swans and pikes as a reward to his brother, the Duke of Gloucester (later Richard III). The City of York agreed that 'the Duke of Gloucester shall, for his grete labor now late made unto ye King's good grace for the co[n]f[or]mac[i]on of the lib[er]ties of þis Citie, be p[rese]nted, at his comyng to the Citie, w[ith] vj swannes and vj pikes.'[24]

Medieval account books are peppered with references to gifts of swans. During Antony Bek's episcopate, Durham Priory Manorial Accounts (c.1285–6) detail: 'Ex quibus in expensis domini Edmundi, ij cingni' (Of expenditure, Master Edmund, two swans).[25] As the manorial accounts contain no reference to a monk named Edmund, the swans may possibly be a gift to the youngest son of Edward I, Edmund of Woodstock (1301–30), possibly at the celebration of his birth. Ties between the two courts were strong: Edward I was Bek's patron, and Bek is thought to have attended the Feast of the Swan held by Edward I in 1306.

Another account, this time from Durham Enrolled Manors in Muggleswick (1296–7), notes: 'Et de ij cingnis de missione Iohannis le Flemeng' (And two swans of John the Fleming's sending).[26] As John the Fleming was a landowner in Newcastle, these swans could be gifts to Durham Priory or rendered payment. Swans also served as a formal apology. When the Burgess of Lydd opened a love-letter belonging to Sir Reginald (a former parish priest), swans were sent to Dover Castle, to the Clerk of the Exchequer, to the Archbishop of Canterbury, and to the mayor of Dover in order 'to secure their friendship'.[27] Because of their worth, swans were also bestowed in wills. In her will (1480–1), Dame Margaret Paston left her grandson Robert 'all my swannes marked with the marke known as Dawbeney's mark'.[28] Other examples are found in the wills of Edmund Hogan (1498), Stephen Iderykke (1507), Robert Robyn (1551), and Malyn Harte (1559).[29]

SWAN KEEPING

Owning and keeping swans was profitable thanks to their value. Swans could be kept in several ways. Sometimes they were kept in a domestic flock on a moat or lake, with wings likely clipped. Swans were likely kept in this manner for priories and manors. Detailed records were kept of the number, usage, and death of swans. The Pittington Records (1304–5) of the Durham Priory Manorial Accounts list their flock in their year-end report:

{Cigni} Idem respondet de xj cignis de remanencia. Et de xiiij de exitu eorundem. Summa, xxv. De quibus in expensis prioris, j. In perdicione, j. Summa expensarum, ij. Et remanent xxiij cygni.

{Swans} Item responding of the 11 swans remaining. And of fourteen on exit of the same [year]. Total, 25. Of those in expense to the priory, 1. In death, 1. Total expenses, 2. And 23 swans remaining.[30]

The high worth of swans necessitated close record-keeping of their numbers. Their deaths – through illness, injury, or accident – were costly. Priory Accounts, such as Durham's, include the cost of feeding swans, emphasising their domestication.[31] A vestige of swan domestication may be seen at The Great Hospital in Norwich, which contains remnants of a large swan pit used to house and feed medieval swans.[32]

Perhaps the more usual method to keep swans was through semi-domestication. Swan owners allowed their swans to wander on commons and in private lands, and to mate and nest on rivers, marshes, fens, and moors. Swans were hunted or gathered as required, and this practice is depicted in 'The Otter and Swan Hunt' in the Devonshire Hunting Tapestries.[33]

SWAN MARKING

Ownership of swans was often contested. Swans roaming freely could easily move to neighbouring land and be claimed by others. To solve this, marking swans became a custom both in Britain and on the Continent.[34] Similar to branding cattle, a mark was cut into the swan's bill to identify the swan as the owner's property. The swan would be turned loose to mate, nest, and rear young. Once a year, swans were caught and any cygnets received their owner's distinctive mark (Figures 16–17).

The practice of catching and marking swans became known as 'swan-upping'. Marking swans was accomplished through the use of a penknife or sometimes a branding iron.[35] Often reflecting their owner, swan marks might consist of heraldic symbols, a merchant's mark, or relate to the owner's name. Religious houses used markings of a prior's or an abbot's staff.[36] Richard Flower of Ely had the mark of the *fleur-de-lys*; and the mark of Sir William Bowes was two *bows* (emphasis mine).[37] Generally the mark was placed upon the swan's upper mandible, but could also occur as notches on its feet.[38] The oldest recorded swan mark *c.*1370 belonged to Sir Richard de Totesham, of West Farleigh, Kent (Figure 16, mark no. 1).[39] But marking swans appears to predate 1370. The Close Rolls of 1246 refer to the seizure of seven cygnets, as one parent was owned by the King and the other by the Hospital of Hampton.[40] A mark would have been essential to identify the swans' different owners. The Patent Rolls of 1276 record that a thief not only stole swans in Norfolk, but also removed their owner's marks.[41]

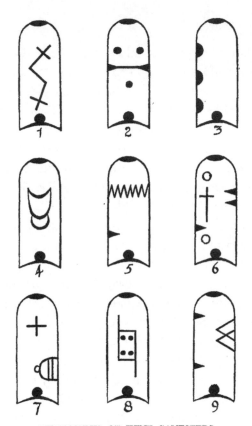

SWAN-MARKS OF KENT GAMESTERS.

Figure 16: English Swan Markings, c.1370–1586; illustration by Norman Ticehurst, 'The Mute Swan in Kent', Archaeologia Cantiana, 47 (1935), 55–70 (pp. 68–9). Public domain. In a selected sample, these swan marks belong to: (1) Sir Richard de Totesham c.1370, possibly the oldest recorded swan mark; (2) The Archbishop of Canterbury; (3) Sir William Boleyn (d. 1505), father of Queen Anne Boleyn, second wife to Henry VIII; (9) William Roper (d. 1578), father-in-law to Sir Thomas More, author of Utopia.

SWANHERDS

Landowners found it expedient to employ swanherds – one who tends or keeps swans. The Parliamentary Rolls of 1482 mention 'Divers Swanherdes, and Kepers of Swannes', but the Durham Priory accounts mention 'swanherds' well before the fourteenth century.[42] A swanherd protected swans: he warded off swan theft, saw that dogs did not injure swans or their nests, and ensured that waters were not disturbed to harm nesting swans.

Swans were frequently stolen due to their worth and their relative accessibility on common land. In the Patent Rolls, an entry on 24 October 1314 recorded a complaint by John, Bishop of Bath and Wells, against those who felled his trees, stole his rabbits, and carried away two broods of swans, and five other swans valued at £10.[43] A commission was issued on 12 February 1365 from Westminster by Edward III and accused four named persons of hunting deer, fish, hares, conies, partridges and pheasants, as well as carrying 'away fish and 100 brood swans and other swans, worth 100l. [£100]'.[44] This was a costly loss. Swan theft was so common that Ticehurst writes 'practically all such entries in the Patent Rolls for this period [1250–1480] include swan stealing as part of the offence'.[45] Swan theft was not the only problem. Thieves might resort to changing or augmenting swan marks. In 1276 in Norfolk, thieves stole swans and removed the swan mark of the owner.[46]

SWAN MASTERS

Royalty went to great lengths to protect their swans. In 1355 Edward, the Black Prince (1330–76), appointed two helpers to guard his swans from theft. Nicholas de Mideford and Simon de Biflet, under the supervision of Thomas Gerveys, were employed to keep the Prince's swans on the Thames between Oxford and London.[47] Thomas Gerveys appears to be the Senior Swanherd under royal directive to keep swans – and may be the first example of a Royal Swan Master. The first definite appointment of a Swan Master was by Edward III on 3 May 1361 to Thomas de Russham: 'Know ye that we have granted to our well-beloved and high-born Thomas de Russham the supervision and custody of all our swans as well in the water of Thames as elsewhere within our Kingdom for as long as it shall be our pleasure.'[48] The Swan Master's full title was the Master of the King's (or Queen's) Game of Swans. He was also referred to as the Royal Swanherd or Chief Swannerd. In addition to caring for royal swans, the Swan Master oversaw swan-keeping throughout England.[49] He maintained royal rights to swans, cared for swan preservation, and safeguarded the rights of swan-owners.[50]

Yet the appointments of the Swan Master, their deputies, and regional swanherds was not enough to reduce the problem of swan thefts. In 1463 King Edward IV issued two commissions to enquire into irregular swan-keeping practices along the Thames and Fenland. Named officers were given the privilege:

> to enquire by oath of good men of the counties of Kent, Hertford, Essex, Surrey, Middlesex, Berks, Buckingham, Oxford and Gloucester into the capture of swans and cygnets on the river Thames and its tributaries from

Cirencestre to its mouth by hooks, nets, 'lymestrynges' and other engines and the taking of swans' eggs, and to arrest and imprison the offenders.[51]

This enquiry into misconduct indicates how swans and their eggs were being stolen. The punishment for swan tampering is severe: arrest and imprisonment. Similar commissions were reissued in 1468, 1470, 1472, and 1477.

SWAN LAWS

Perhaps as a result of these commissions, Edward IV issued *The Act for Swans* in 1482. The injury was that some 'have stolen Cygnets and put upon them their own mark, by which unlawful means the substance of Swans be in the hands and possession of Yeomen and Husbandmen, and other persons of little Reputation'.[52] *The Act for Swans* prevented commoners such as yeomen or husbandmen from owning swans, but gave this privilege to either landowners or those with tenements of over five marks per year. The owners of swan marks whose property was below five marks lost out: 'It shall be lawful to any of the King's subjects, having Lands and Tenements to the said value, to seize the said Swans as forfeit, whereof the King shall have one Half, and he that shall seize the other Half'.[53] The law not only deprived the poor of an income, but increased the wealth of the King and landed gentry by seizing swans from the less wealthy.

Legal battles over swans required the introduction of special legal courts called Swan-Motes or Swan courts. These were districted by county and tried by jury. Ticehurst lists the duties of the Swan-Mote jury: 'They were [...] to

enquire into, deal with and award punishments for, trans-
gressions of the swan laws, and to settle disputes between
owners and between owners and the Crown.'[54] The origin of
Swan-Mote is difficult to ascertain, but two previous cases
tried swan misdemeanours by jury. Abbotsbury Manor,
according to their court rolls of 1393, charged the Keeper
of Swans, William Squilor, with stirring up waters besides
the Lord's nesting swans, as well as moving and destroying
swans' eggs.[55] The court ruled that he was in mercy. Another
record in the same year names nine men who, in the words
of Ticehurst, 'put themselves in the mercy of the Lord
because they fished in the Westflete and disturbed and
moved the Swans of the Lord from their eggs to the grave
damage of the Lord as was presented by the 12 Jurors'.[56]

By the reign of Elizabeth I (1533–1603) Swan-Motes
were in regular use. Swan-Motes met in Lincoln (1524), in
Buckinghamshire (1566), and in Cambridgeshire (1575).[57]
One of the more extensively preserved Swan-Motes pro-
ceedings issued from Dorsetshire on 28 February 1596.
Elizabeth I showed great interest in swans. An ordinance of
1581 enquired on her behalf as to why her breeding swans
in Lincolnshire were reduced from ninety to six. The Swan-
Mote was charged to find 'what has become of the said old
swannes and what person or persons do conceal or with-
hold the same and by what means'.[58]

Swan ownership became increasingly restricted after
The Act for Swans was passed in 1482. Edward IV's undated
Proclamation between 1547 and 1553 introduced more
swan laws to the Fenland. Swan marking had to occur in the
presence of the king's swanherd or deputy.[59] Sale and deliv-
ery of swans had to be made in the presence of or with the

permission of the Master Swanherd or his deputy and four other swanherds. Any person who harmed swans' nests or destroyed or took swans' eggs was to be charged fourteen shillings and four pence (14/ 4d) per egg. The Proclamation outlawed dog-hunting of swans between Easter and Trinity; demanded snares be removed between Easter and Lammas; and banned the use of nets between the Feast of the Holy Cross and Lammas.

Elizabeth I exercised ever greater control over swans. She reissued Edward IV's Swan Proclamation in 1563–4 and enlarged its scope. In 1584–5, she issued 'The Order for Swannes'. In it, she moved to unify swan laws and augment the Crown's power. The owners of swan marks now had to pay the Crown for that privilege – a one-time charge that enabled them to keep swans for their entire life. Stronger punishments were enforced for those who harmed breeding swans:

> Also if any person or persons doo driue awai any Swan or Swannes bréeding or prouiding to bréede, be it vpon his owne ground or any other mans ground, hée or they so offending shall suffer one yeares imprisonment, and fine at the Quéenes pleasure, thirtéene shillings foure pence.[60]

Altering a swan mark carried the penalty of a year's imprisonment and a fine. Carrying a swan-hook – a device used to catch swans – also incurred a fine, as did the theft of swan eggs.

James I (1566–1625) tightened swan laws even further. His expanded *The Order for Swannes* (1615–20) included tighter administration surrounding swanherds and banned the handling of unmarked swans, except on upping days.[61] Those who inherited swan marks had to pay six shillings, eight pence to enrol their swan mark, and to keep their mark, swan owners now had to pay four shillings each year. Stricter provisions were made around the date of swan marking. If anyone was caught marking swans outside this period, his mark was forfeited to the King and for every swan marked, he was fined forty shillings. The fine for dogs killing a swan was also forty shillings.

Under Charles I's reign, *The Orders, Laws and Ancient Customes of Swanns* (1632) set further limitations on swans. The most important is this: 'Also all Swannes that are cleare of Bill, without marke or signe marke, are the Kings onely, whether they be pinioned or flying Swannes'.[62] All un-marked swans became, by default, the property of the Crown, including stray swans or those with an unidentifiable mark. This law is still in effect in England today. Other laws instituted by the 1632 ordinance clarify the ownership of cygnets:

> In all Common streames and priuate waters when Cignets are taken vp, the owner of the Cob must chuse the first Cignet, and the Pen the next, and so in order. But if there be three, then the owner of the Grasse where they breed, must haue the third, for the spoyle of his Grasse.[63]

As swans roamed somewhat freely, and as one swan might breed with a swan owned by another, disputes over ownership of cygnets arose. The 1632 Ordinance placed an emphasis on the Swan Master's Register Book, where he was charged to record the number of swans and 'the place where they are vpt'.[64]

SWAN UPPING

Disputes over swan-ownership increased the importance of swan marking. Every swan-mark owner was required to attend the annual Swan Upping with the Royal Swanherd or his deputy. Swan Upping usually occurred on the Monday after St Peter's Day (roughly between 30 June–6 July). Breeding swans were caught, and their marks were examined and checked against the Record of Swan Marks that

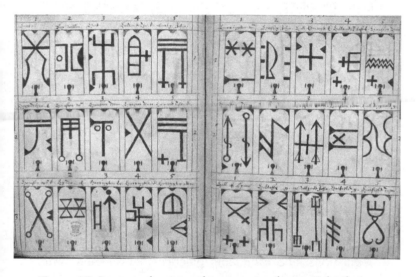

Figure 17: *Swan marks, sixteenth century. London, British Library, MS Harley 3405, fos 18v–19 © British Library Board. Swan Rolls, such as these, were used to register personal swan marks. Swan Uppings occurred annually, where the Swanherd and his deputies would 'up' or catch swans and compare their markings to the official register. Only registered swan markings were allowed and owning a swan mark became increasingly costly.*

the Royal Swanherd possessed. Both the Royal and regional Swanherds had registers of swan marks. These were written on parchment rolls, depicted all swan marks used within the district, and indicated the owner's name and the upkeep of his fees. Between sixty-seventy of these documents, called Swan Rolls, have been preserved (Figure 16–17).[65]

The Royal Swanherd had a second book, called the Upping Book. Renewed annually, the Upping Book detailed the location of swan broods, the number of cygnets, their mark, the name of the owner of each parent-bird, and to whom the cygnets were allocated. A record of 1587 reads: 'Uppid in the fulling mil Rever j brode of S., the cok mis basye the hen mr bennitts' (Upped in the Fulling Mill River one brood of swans, the cock Mistress Basshe's, the hen M'. Bennett's).[66]

LEGACIES OF SWAN OWNERSHIP

Over the course of the early modern period, swan owner-ship became increasingly restricted, increasingly costly, and increasingly monitored. Swan rights were contested until the early 1800s, when turkeys became the preferred dinner bird.[67] As eating swans became less popular, the rituals, regulations, and ownership practices surrounding swans were gradually abandoned. However, vestiges of these ancient traditions remain in England today. The Monarch still owns all unmarked swans in England. The right to own swans was granted to many Oxford colleges. Reportedly, Fellows of St John's College were granted the privilege to consume unmarked swans – with swan traps built into the college walls along the Isis (Thames). However, swan rights for Oxford colleges appear to have lapsed. Two medieval guilds – or trades companies – purchased swan marks: the Vintners' Company (wine merchants) and the Dyers' Company (cloth-dying merchants). Ticehurst mentions that David Selby, Master of the Vintners' Company 1439–40, owned a swan mark.[68] It is likely he devised the Vintners' swan mark of a long 'V', or 'two nicks', upon the bill. Between 1472–83, the Company received swan-rights from the Crown and were known to exercise their rights from 1509. The Vintners' Livery Company used this mark for centuries. Today those with swan-rights include the Vintners' Company, the Dyers' Company, and the Ilchester Family of Abbotsbury. Few apart from the Monarch have the right to own swans.

SWANSONG
THE AFTERLIVES
OF THE
MEDIEVAL SWAN

BECAUSE OF the swan's importance to medieval culture, it is little wonder that its afterlives rippled across the centuries. This extends to art, poetry, prose, film, ballet, music, the law, opera, architecture, idioms, and pub signs.

SWANSONG AND TRANSFORMATION

Shakespeare, Spencer, Tennyson, Coleridge – all refer to the swan's dying song in their literary works.[1] The phrase 'swansong' acquired its modern meaning through Franz Schubert. His last great piece was *Schwanengesang* (Swan Song), composed in 1828 just before his death. Schubert's *Schwanengesang* was viewed as his swansong – his last great work of genius – a definition employed by Cicero. From here 'swansong' gained its more popular meaning, defined by the Oxford English Dictionary as 'the last work of a poet or musician, composed shortly before his death; hence, any final performance, action, or effort'.[2] In recent memory, this might be Heath Ledger's final performance as the Joker in *The Dark Knight* (2008), dying before it was released in cinema, and winning, posthumously, an Oscar for his performance. Swansongs frequently apply to athletics, such as when English cricketer Sir Alastair Cook announced his retirement, and in his final test match, knowing it to be his last, scored 147 runs.

Since the Renaissance, Leda and the Swan has been a favourite artistic theme of heightened sensuality and (deviant) amorous desire.[3] Those depicting Leda and the Swan have included Michelangelo (*c*.1529, lost), Leonardo da Vinci (*c*.1504, lost), Correggio (*c*.1530), François Boucher (1740), Paul Cézanne (*c*.1882), and Salvador Dalí (1949). In 2012, the Metropolitan Police instructed that a portrait of Leda and the Swan be removed from view in the Scream Gallery for illustrating bestiality – a punishable offence.[4] Both Michelangelo's and Leonardo's paintings were likely destroyed for similar reasons. 'Leda and the Swan' is also the title of Yeats's famous poem (1924).

The swan's transformative potential continues. In Grimm's *Fairy Tales* (1812), a sister disenchants her six brothers who had been transformed into swans.[5] In Tchaikovsky's famous ballet, *Swan Lake* (1875–6), the sorcerer Rothbart transforms Princess Odette into a white swan and his own daughter Odile (Odette's rival) into a black swan. The ballet inspired the Disney film *The Swan Princess* (1994) where the princess is a swan by day and a human by moonlight. Adapted from *Swan Lake*, the Award-Winning film *Black Swan* (2010) rehearses medieval views of swans. The bestiary swan – depicted as duplicitous, layered, and hiding something beneath its pure exterior – fits well with the movie's themes of doppelgängers and tenuous reality. The film embodies a literal swansong as Nina gives her best and final performance as the swans in *Swan Lake*, a performance so life-giving that it directly results in her death at the ballet's end.

Later composers have brought to life medieval renditions of swansongs. Carl Orff set to music thirty songs found in the *Carmina Burana* including *Olim lacus* (1935–6).[6] The simple medieval tune of *Clangam, filii* has been notated and sung in choral arrangements.[7] The poet-as-swan, stemming from classical texts, also continues. Coined by Ben Jonson, Shakespeare was known as the 'Swan-of-Avon'.[8]

NATURAL HISTORY, CONSERVATION, AND THE CROWN

The swan's current natural history focuses on data acquisition surrounding its migration, habitat, reproduction, diet, and parental behaviour. Due to the dramatic decline of swans in Britain in the 1970s, the focus has turned to swan conservation. For a time, their leading cause of death was lead fishing weights, accidentally consumed. These are now outlawed in Britain.[9] Under the Wildlife and Conservation Act of 1981 (UK), harming a swan is punishable by six months imprisonment and/or a fine.

Swan Upping still occurs on the third Monday in July. This too now focuses on conservation. Both the Vintners' and Dyers' Companies accompany the Queen's Swan Master (now called Swan Marker) as they 'up' swans. They journey over five days between Eton Bridge and Moulsford.[10] They herd swan families, assess swan health, weigh cygnets, and record their numbers, marks, and locations. Vintners' and Dyers' mark their swans through circlets on the swans' ankles. The Queen's swans remain unmarked. Swans are not eaten today, but the Vintners' Company still holds its annual Swan Feast on the Third Thursday of November, where a stuffed swan is presented on a platter.

One of the titles of Queen Elizabeth II is 'Seigneur of the Swans'. She exercises her right to swans only along the Thames. The Queen has upheld the medieval tradition of swans as costly gifts. At the bequest of an American woman stationed in Britain, in 1957 the Queen gifted a pair of breeding swans to the woman's hometown of Lakeland, Florida, where alligators had ravaged their swan population.[11] The gifted swans had many adventures. First a barge spill covered them in oil, and then, after their arrival in Lakeland, their temporary disappearance resulted in a frantic helicopter search. The pair have bred so successfully that Lakeland have sold some of their progeny due to overpopulation.

AFTERLIVES OF THE SWAN KNIGHT

While not well-known in either British or American culture, the Swan Knight legend had a pronounced influence in Germany. Richard Wagner turned the Swan Knight legend into opera with his *Lohengrin* (1848).[12] Basing his opera on the Middle High German medieval *Parzival* and *Lohengrin*, Wagner's Swan Knight rescues Elsa from the false accusation of murdering her brother Gottfried. Wagner's swan also transforms, but it is not an angel. As Lohengrin prepares to depart, he prays over the swan and it transforms into Gottfried, Elsa's missing brother and the rightful Duke of Brabant, cursed into swan-form by the sorceress Ortrud. Wagner's *Lohengrin* was proclaimed as a masterpiece, haunting and unearthly.

The Swan Knight legend shaped German topography in the Schwangau (Swan region) – home to at least three medieval castles associated with swans. Schwangau castle – home to Hiltbolt von Schwangau – was eventually sold to the Lords of Bavaria. Maximilian II of Bavaria (d. 1864) reconstructed this into Hohenschwangau Castle, the official summer and hunting residence of his family.[13] The swan was a leitmotif throughout the palace. The swan was a heraldic emblem of the knights of Schwangau. Seeing himself as their successor, Maximilian adopted their coats of arms – a white swan on red background.[14]

His son, King Ludwig II of Bavaria constructed two other medieval swan-ruins into Neuschwanstein – New Swan Castle. His inspiration for the castle was directly provided by Wagner's *Lohengrin*. He wrote to Wagner in May 1868:

> *Ich habe die Absicht, die alte Burgruine Hohenschwangau bei der Pöllatschlucht neu aufbauen zu lassen im echten Styl der alten deutschen Ritterburgen [...] Auch Reminiszenzen aus 'Tannhäuser' (Sängersaal mit Aussicht auf die Burg im Hintergrunde), aus 'Lohengrin' (Burghof, offener Gang, Weg zur Kapelle) werden Sie dort finden.*

> It is my intention to rebuild the old castle ruin of Hohenschwangau near the Pöllat Gorge in the authentic style of the old German knights' castles [...] It will also remind you of 'Tannhäuser' (Singers' Hall with a view of the castle in the background), 'Lohengrin' (castle courtyard, open corridor, path to the chapel).[15]

Swan decorations permeate Neuschwanstein. They appear in the Schwangau coat of arms, on chandeliers, decorative wash basins, enamel vases, glass doors, and silk coverings for chairs and window seats.[16] In the King's Living room is 'Swan's Corner', a place where 'King Ludwig is said to

Figure 18: *Neuschwanstein Castle, Bayern, c.*1890–1900. Washington, D.C., *Library of Congress Prints and Photographs,* LOT 13411, *no.* 0170.

have particularly liked to sit and read'.[17] Adorning the walls are murals of *Lohengrin*, many depicting the opera's swan. Swans appear on curtains, table and seat coverings, rugs, flower vases, and figurines. Neuschwanstein is likely the most iconic castle known today (Figure 18). It was the inspiration behind Disney's Cinderella Castle that is now the logo of Disney itself.[18]

Besides castles, Wagner's *Lohengrin* inspired the art of the Pre-Raphaelites of the late nineteenth and early twentieth centuries. Walter Crane's *Lohengrin* (1895) is one example, inspired by Wagner's *Lohengrin*, which he attended in Bayreuth (1893). Crane describes the performance, remembering, 'the far-off swan-music [...] reminded one of a creeping mist over the lowlands, or the silver windings of a river flowing ever nearer, until it reached one's feet in full flood'.[19] His painting reflects this very description.

Perhaps the most famous modern rendition of the Swan Knight is one of the most overlooked. The Knights of the Swan are key allies to Minas Tirith in J. R. R. Tolkien's *The Return of the King* (1965). Unlike the *Lord of the Rings* films (2001–3) in which Gondor has few allies, in Tolkien's book Prince Imrahil of Dol Amroth responds to Gondor's summons for help. Last to enter the city before siege was

> Imrahil, Prince of Dol Amroth, kinsman of the Lord, with gilded banners bearing his token of the Ship and the Silver Swan, and a company of knights in full harness riding grey horses; and behind them seven hundreds of men at arms, tall as lords, grey-eyed, dark-haired, singing as they came.[20]

Although written out of the film, Prince Imrahil is a main character in *The Return of the King*. When hounded by the Nazgul, Faramir is rescued by the Swan Knights: 'For foremost on the field rode the swan-knights of Dol Amroth with their Prince and his blue banner at their head. "Amroth for Gondor!" they cried. "Amroth to Faramir!"'[21] The Swan Knights are pivotal in the Battle of Pelennor Fields, and

Prince Imrahil is equal to Aragorn and Éomer: 'Aragon and Éomer and Imrahil rode back [...] few indeed had dared to abide them or look on their faces in the hour of their wrath'.[22] With Denethor dead and Faramir wounded, Prince Imrahil takes temporary stewardship of Minas Tirith. In the final assault against Sauron at the Black Gates stood 'the banners of Rohan and Dol Amroth, White Horse and Silver Swan'.[23] Perhaps like the medieval Swan Knight, who aids Elsa of Brabant in her dire need, so too Prince Imrahil and his Swan Knights provide Gondor with comradeship of allies in their darkest hour.

SWAN IN HERALDRY

The swan as heraldic emblem is still seen today, for example on the town arms of Buckingham. But it is most frequently seen in English pub signs. In medieval Britain, the swan was 'proverbially associated with drinking'.[24] The swan on the hoop was advertisement for the brewer's house. The *Liber Albus* (1419) complains that these signs were so unwieldy that they created road-hazards.[25] 'The Swan' is currently one of the top five pub names in England.[26] The most common pub name is 'The White Hart'. The badges that so plagued Richard II's reign – the swan and white hart – still circulate today. The Swan Hotel in the little town of Wadebridge has a rather beautiful sign, featuring a Mute Swan with a golden crown on its neck attached to a golden chain. Little though passers-by may be aware, that crowned swan ultimately harks back to the swan with a magical, costly necklace which he used to draw his brother, the Swan Knight, in boat. Thanks to the nobility of medieval Europe vying for Swan Knight ancestry, this ducally gorged swan became a heraldic device, and was eventually popularised throughout England as the emblem of the Lancasters. This little pub sign reflects a swathe of medieval cultural history and demonstrates just one way in which the medieval swan inflitrates modern life, although the reason for its presence is almost lost in time immemorial.

ENDNOTES

INTRODUCTION

1. Jeremy Mynott, *Birds in the Ancient World* (Oxford: Oxford University Press, 2018), pp. 214–15.
2. A. J. Parker, 'The Birds of Roman Britain', *Oxford Journal of Archaeology*, 7/2 (1988), 197–226.
3. For the following, see Stanley Cramp, et al. (eds), *Handbook of the Birds of Europe, the Middle East, and North Africa: The Birds of the Western Palearctic, Volume 1: Ostrich to Ducks* (Oxford: Oxford University Press, 2005); and Janet Kear (ed.), *Ducks, Geese and Swans*, vol. 1 (Oxford: Oxford University Press, 2005).
4. For the following, see Cramp, et al., *Handbook*, pp. 379–85; Kear, *Ducks, Geese and Swans*, pp. 243–8; Myrfyn Owen, *Wildfowl of Europe* (London: Macmillan, 1977), pp. 84–91; H. F. Witherby, F. C. R. Jourdain, Norman F. Ticehurst, and Bernard W. Tucker (eds), *The Handbook of British Birds*, vol. 3 (London: H. F. & G. Witherby, 1840), pp. 172–4.
5. For the following see, Cramp et al., *Handbook*, pp. 385–91; Kear, *Ducks*, pp. 249–56; Owen, *Wildfowl*, pp. 78–84; Witherby et al., *British Birds*, pp. 168–72.
6. Witherby et al., *British Birds*, p. 169; Jean Delacour, *Waterfowl of the World*, vol. 4 (London: Country Life Limited, 1964), pp. 169–201;

Paul A. Johnsgard, *Handbook of Waterfowl Behavior* (London: Constable & Co., 1965), pp. 25, 32; Cramp et al., *Handbook*, p. 389.

7. For the following see Cramp et al., *Handbook*, pp. 370–9; Kear, *Ducks*, pp. 231–4; Owen, *Wildfowl*, pp. 70–8; Witherby et al., *British Birds*, pp. 174–9; and Mike Birkhead and Christopher Perrins, *The Mute Swan* (London: Croom Helm 1986). Polish Swans, or *Cygnus olor morpha immutabilis*, also exist in Europe, but are classified as a genetic mutation of the Mute Swan. Carrying a copy of the gene responsible for 'leucism', the Polish Swan is lighter in colour than the Mute Swan, with pinkish legs and bill, rather than black, and its cygnets are off-white. For more see Moss Taylor, 'The Polish swan in Britain & Ireland', *British Birds*, 111 (2018): 10–24.

I   THE SWAN'S SONG

1. Isidore of Seville, *Etymologiarum sive originum libri XX*, ed. W. M. Lindsay, 2 vols (Oxford: Clarendon Press, 1911); tr. Stephen A. Barney, W. J. Lewis, J. A. Beach, and Oliver Berghof (Cambridge: Cambridge University Press, 2006), XII.7.18–19.

2. Mynott, *Birds*, p. 57.

3. Mynott, *Birds*, p. 57; Willene B. Clark, *A Medieval Book of Beasts: The Second-Family Bestiary* (Woodbridge: Boydell Press, 2006), p. 171 n. 247.

4. Aelian, *On the Characteristics of Animals*, ed. and tr. A. F. Scholfield, 3 vols (Cambridge, MA: Harvard University Press, 1959), vol. 2, XI.1 (pp. 356–9).

5. See Frederick M. Ahl, 'Amber, Avallon, and Apollo's Singing Swan', *The American Journal of Philology*, 103/4 (1982), 373–411; P. R. Hardie, 'Aeneas and the Omen of the Swans (Verg. Aen. I. 393–400)', *Classical Philology*, 82/2 (1987), 145–50; D'Arcy Wentworth Thompson, *A Glossary of Greek Birds* (London: Oxford University Press, 1936), pp. 179–86.

6. Plato, *Phaedo*, in *Euthyphro, Apology, Crito, Phaedo, Phaedrus*, ed. and tr. Harold North Fowler (London: William Heinemann, 1926), 84e–85b (pp. 294–5).

7. Aeschylus, *Agamemnon*, in *Oresteia*, ed. and tr. Hugh Lloyd-Jones (London: William Heinemann, 1971), ll. 1444–5 (pp. 128–9), with minor adjustments.

8. Moschus, 'Lament for Bion', in *Theocritus, Moschus, Bion*, ed. and tr. Neil Hopkinson (Cambridge, MA: Harvard University Press, 2015), ll. 14–15 (pp. 468–9).

9. Aristotle, *History of Animals: Books* VII–X, ed. and tr. D. M. Balme (Cambridge, MA: Harvard University Press, 1991), VIII.12.615b (pp. 272–3).

10. Cicero, *De Oratore*, ed. and tr. H. Rackham, 2 vols (London: William Heinemann, 1942), III.2.6 (pp. 6–7).

11. Ovid, *Metamorphoses*, ed. and tr. Frank Justus Miller, 2 vols (London: William Heinemann, 1968), XIV.428–30 (pp. 330–1); tr. Anthony S. Kline (Ann Arbor: Borders Classics, 2004), XIV.397–434. Future references are to Miller's edition, unless specified otherwise.

12. Virgil, *Aeneid*: VII–XII, ed. and tr. H. Rushton Fairclough, 2 vols (London: William Heinemann, 1986), VII.700–701 (pp. 50–1).

13. Aesop, *The Complete Fables*, tr. Olivia and Robert Temple (London: Penguin, 1998), 173, 174.

14. Sylvia Bruce Wilmore, *Swans of the World* (New York: Taplinger Publishing Co., 1974), p. 216.

15. Ahl, 'Singing Swan', p. 373; Eratosthenes and Hyginus, *Constellation Myths with Aratus's Phaenomena*, tr. Robin Hard (Oxford: Oxford University Press, 2015), pp. 20–6.

16. Pliny, *Natural History, Volume* III: *Books* 8–11, ed. and tr. H. Rackham (London: William Heinemann, 1940), X.32.63 (pp. 332–3).

17. Lactantius, *Phoenix*, in *Minor Latin Poets*, ed. and tr. J. Wight Duff and Arnold M. Duff (London: William Heinemann, 1934), l. 50 (pp. 654–5).

18. Heraclius, *Sermo Augustino praesente*, P.L. XXXIX:1717. Unless specified, translations are mine.

19. Origenes, 'In Canticum Canticorum', in *Origenes Werke: Homilién zu Samuel I, zum Hohelied und zu den Propheten Kommentar zum Hohelied*, ed. W. A. Baehrens (Leipzig: J. C. Hinrich, 1925), Liber III (p. 208); tr. in *Physiologus: A Medieval Book of Nature Lore*, tr. Michael J. Curley (Chicago: University of Chicago Press, 2009), p. xiii.

20. Clark, *Book of Beasts*, p. 14.

21. See A. C. Crombie, *Augustine to Galileo: Volume I, Science in the Middle Ages*, V–XIII *Centuries* (London: William Heinemann, 1957), pp. 75–98; C. S. Lewis, *The Discarded Image: An Introduction to Medieval and Renaissance Literature* (Cambridge: Cambridge University Press, 1964); Corinne Saunders, *Magic and the Supernatural in Medieval English Romance* (Cambridge: Boydell and Brewer, 2010), pp. 31–4.

22. Rabanus Maurus, *De Universo*, VIII.vi, PL 111:245b–245c; tr. Priscilla Throop, 2 vols (Charlotte, VT: Medieval MS, 2009), vol. 1, VIII.vi (p. 264).

23. *Physiologus*, tr. Curley, pp. ix–xxxiii.

24. Clark, *Book of Beasts*, pp. 8–20.

25. See D. L. D'Avray, *The Preaching of the Friars: Sermons Diffused from Paris before* 1300 (Oxford: Clarendon Press, 1985), pp. 232–3.

26. For second-family bestiaries, see Clark's *Books of Beasts*, pp. 171–2; and T. H. White, *The Book of Beasts: Being a Translation from a Latin Bestiary of the Twelfth Century* (London: Jonathan Cape, 1954), pp. 118–19. See also Florence McCulloch, *Medieval Latin and French Bestiaries* (Chapel Hill: University of North Carolina Press, 1962), p. 176; and Wilma George and Brunsdon Yapp, *The Naming of the Beasts* (London: Duckworth, 1991).

27. Hugh of Fouilloy, *The Medieval Book of Birds: Hugh of Fouilloy's Aviarium*, ed. and tr. Willene B. Clark (Binghamton, NY: Medieval & Renaissance Texts & Studies, 1992), pp. 10–12.

28. Hugh of Fouilloy, *Aviarium*, 58, pp. 240–5 (pp. 242–3). Subsequent references follow this edition with minor adjustments.

29. Baudouin Van den Abeele, 'Trente et un nouveaux manuscrits de l'*Aviarium*: regards sur la diffusion de l'œuvre d'Hugues de Fouilloy', *Scriptorium*, 57/2 (2003), 253–71; Hugh of Fouilloy, *Aviarium*, pp. xi, 21–6.
30. *Bestiary: Being an English Version of the Bodleian Library, Oxford, MS Bodley 764*, tr. Richard Barber (Woodbridge: Boydell Press, 1999), p. 134.
31. Cramp et al., *Handbook*, pp. 372–9; Kear, *Ducks*, p. 231.
32. Elizabeth Morrison, *Book of Beasts: The Bestiary in the Medieval World* (Los Angeles: The J. Paul Getty Museum, 2019), p. 113.
33. Carolyn Muessig, 'The Sermones Friales et Communes of Jacques de Vitry . . . Part 1', *Medieval Sermon Studies*, 47/1 (2003), 33–49 (p. 48).
34. Chaucer, 'The Summoner's Tale', in *The Riverside Chaucer*, ed. Larry D. Benson (Oxford: Oxford University Press, 1987), pp. 129–36 (ll. 1930–1). Different readings exist between 'swan' or 'swain'. See Daniel S. Silvia, Jr., 'Chaucer's Friars, Swans or Swains? *Summoner's Tale*, D 1930', *English Language Notes*, 1 (1964), 248–50.
35. Beryl Rowland, *Birds with Human Souls: A Guide to Bird Symbolism* (Knoxville: University of Tennessee Press, 1978), p. 171.
36. *The Quest of the Holy Grail*, tr. P. M. Matarasso (Middlesex: Penguin, 1969), pp. 183–4.
37. *La Queste del Saint Graal*, ed. Albert Pauphilet (Paris: Édouard Champion, 1923), pp. 185–6; tr. Matarasso, p. 198.
38. *Physiologus*, tr. Curley, pp. 9–10; Morrison, *Book of Beasts*, p. 192.
39. Paris, Bibliothèque nationale de France, Bibliothèque de l'Arsenal, MS 3516, fol. 207r; following Rowland, *Human Souls*, p. 171.
40. *The Tretyse of Loue*, ed. John H. Fisher (London: Oxford University Press, 1951), p. 112.
41. Alexander Neckam, *De Naturis Rerum*, ed. Thomas Wright (London: Longman, Green, Longman, Roberts, and Green, 1863), XLIX (p. 101); tr. Rowland, *Human Souls*, p. 171.

42. Crombie, *Augustine to Galileo*, p. 6.

43. Kellie Robertson, *Nature Speaks: Medieval Literature and Aristotelian Philosophy* (Philadelphia: University of Pennsylvania Press, 2017), p. 92; and Clark, *Book of Beasts*, pp. 14–15.

44. Batholomaeus Anglicus, *On the Properties of Things: John Trevisa's Translation of Bartholomaeus Anglicus De Proprietatibus Rerum*, ed. M. C. Seymour, 3 vols (Oxford: Clarendon Press, 1975), XII (p. 632).

45. Birkhead and Perrins, *Mute Swan*, p. 9; Cramp et al., *Handbook*, pp. 376–7.

46. Thomas of Cantimpré, *Liber de Natura Rerum*, ed. Helmut Boese, 2 vols (Berlin: Walter de Gruyter, 1973), vol. 1, V.26 (pp. 188–9).

47. Swans belong to Kingdom Animalia, Phylum Chordata, Class Aves, Order Anseriformes, Family Anatidae, Subfamily Anserinae, Genus Cygnus.

48. The following section refers to, Albertus Magnus, *De Animalibus*: XIII–XXVI, ed. Hermann Stadler, *Beiträge zur Geschichte der Philosophie des Mittelalters* XXVI (Münster: Aschendorffschen, 1920), XXIII.22 (pp. 1447–8); *On Animals: A Medieval Summa Zoologica*, tr. Kenneth F. Kitchell Jr. and Irven Michael Resnick, 2 vols (Columbus: Ohio State University Press, 2018), XXIII.22 (pp. 1564–5). See also Cramp et al., *Handbook*, pp. 375, 387–8.

49. Albertus Magnus, *On Animals*, XXIII.22 (p. 1448); tr. Kitchell and Resnick (p. 1565).

50. Cramp et al., *Handbook*, pp. 376–7; Paul Johnsgard, *Swans: Their Biology and Natural History* (Lincoln: University of Nebraska Press, 2016), pp. 16–19.

51. Albertus Magnus, *On Animals*, XXIII.22 (p. 1447); tr. Kitchell and Resnick (p. 1565).

52. Cramp et al., *Handbook*, p. 372.

53. Henry Seebohm, *A History of British Birds: Volume Three* (London: R. H. Porter, 1885), p. 477.

54. Thomas Aquinas, *Summa Theologiae, Volume 29*, ed. Thomas Gilby (London: Eyre and Spottiswoode, 1969) 1a2ae. 102, 6 (pp. 218–19).

55. Owen, *Wildfowl*, p. 70.
56. Alan of Lille, *The Plaint of Nature*, in *Literary Works*, ed. and tr. Winthrop Wetherbee (Cambridge, MA: Harvard University Press, 2013), II.21 (pp. 40–1).
57. Latin (expanded) from digitised Oxford, Bodleian Library, MS. Bodley 764; tr. Barber, *Bestiary*, p. 135.
58. Vincent of Beauvais, *Speculum Naturale* (Venice: Hermannus Liechtenstein, 1494), XXXIII.1 (p. 406).
59. Thomas of Cantimpré, *De natura rerum*, V.26 (p. 188).
60. Albertus Magnus, *On Animals*, XXIII.22, tr. Kitchell and Resnick (p. 1565) with minor adjustments.
61. Ranee Katzenstein and Emilie Savage-Smith, *The Leiden Aratea: Ancient Constellations in a Medieval Manuscript* (Malibu: J. Paul Getty Museum, 1988), pp. 28–9; Eratosthenes and Hyginus, *Constellation Myths*, pp. 20–6.
62. Thomas of Cantimpré, *De natura rerum*, V.26 (p. 188).
63. Florence McCulloch, 'The Dying Swan – A Misunderstanding', *Modern Language Notes*, 74/4 (1959), 289–92.
64. McCulloch, 'The Dying Swan', 289–92; Ovid, *Fasti*, and and tr. James George Frazer (London: William Heinemann, 1931), II.109–10 (pp. 64–5).
65. Cramp et al., *Handbook*, p. 377.
66. Mynott, *Birds*, pp. 53–5.
67. Parker, 'Roman Britain', pp. 197–226.
68. Dieter Bitterli, *Say What I Am Called: The Old English Riddles of the Exeter Book and the Anglo-Latin Riddle Tradition* (Toronto: University of Toronto Press, 2009), pp. 35–56 (p. 44).
69. *The Exeter Book*, ed. George Philip Krapp and Elliott van Kirk Dobbie, *Anglo-Saxon Poetic Records*, vol. 3 (London: George Routledge, 1936), pp. 184–5; tr. Bitterli, *Say What*, p. 40.
70. Craig Williamson, *Old English Riddles of the Exeter Book* (Chapel Hill: University of North Carolina Press, 1977), pp. 72, 151.
71. Cramp et al., *Handbook*, pp. 372, 377.

72. David Cabot, *Wildfowl* (London: Collins, 2009), p. 40.

73. *Homeric Hymn*, xxx 1–2, following Mynott, *Birds*, p. 54.

74. Aristophanes, *Birds*, 769–73, following Mynott, *Birds*, p. 54.

75. PG XXXVII:212, following Williamson, *Riddles of the Exeter Book*, p. 152.

76. Peter Godman, *Poetry of the Carolingian Renaissance* (London: Duckworth, 1985), pp. 69–71, 322–5. All references follow this edition with minor adjustments.

77. Albertus Magnus, *On Animals*, XXIII.22.

78. For a Christian interpretation, see Ricarda Liver, 'Der singende Schwan: Motivgeschichtliches zu einer Sequenz des 9. Jahrhunderts', *Museum Helveticum*, 39/1 (1982), 146–56; and Godman, *Poetry*, pp. 69–71. For a secular one, see Peter Dronke, 'The Beginnings of the Sequence', *Beiträg zur Geschichte der deutschen Sprache und Literatur*, 87 (1965), 43–73; and John Stevens, *Words and Music in the Middle Ages* (Cambridge: Cambridge University Press, 1986), pp. 110–14 (p. 113).

79. Godman, *Poetry*, pp. 69–70.

80. Stevens, *Words and Music*, p. 113; Godman, *Poetry*, p. 71.

81. Stevens, *Words and Music*, p. 112.

82. Helen Leaf, 'English Medieval Bone Flutes: A Brief Introduction', *The Galpin Society Journal*, 59 (2006), 13–19.

83. Cramp et al., *Handbook*, pp. 380, 383.

84. Cramp et al., *Handbook*, p. 389.

85. Delacour, *Waterfowl*, pp. 197–8; Johnsgard, *Waterfowl Behavior*, p. 32; Cramp et al., *Handbook*, p. 389.

86. In example, see Washington Irving, *Astoria or Anecdotes of an Enterprise beyond the Rocky Mountains*, 2 vols (New York: George P. Putnam, 1849), vol. 1, p. 13.

87. Swan numbers have certainly dropped. See Simon Delany, Jeremy J. D. Greenwood, and Jeff Kirby, 'National Mute Swan Survey 1990', *Report to the Joint Nature Conservation Committee* (February, 1992).

88. Cramp et al., *Handbook*, p. 371.

89. Andreas R. Pfenning et al., 'Convergent Transcriptional Specializations in the Brains of Humans and Song-learning Birds', *Science*, 346/6215 (12 December 2014), DOI: 10.1126/science.1256846.

90. As we have seen, viewpoints on natural history change over time. Focusing on trends across species, Kear writes, swans 'do not sing in the true sense and certainly not just before they die', from *Mute Swan*, following A. Lindsay Price, *Swans of the World: In Nature, History, Myth & Art* (Tulsa: Council Oak Books, 1994), p. 52.

91. For convoluted trachea, see Johnsgard, *Waterfowl Behavior*, p. 32; Witherby et al., *British Birds*, p. 169; Delacour, *Waterfowl*, pp. 197–8; Cramp et al., *Handbook*, p. 389.

92. Cramp et al., *Handbook*, p. 389.

93. Witherby et al., *British Birds*, p. 169.

94. W. Geoffrey Arnott, 'Swan Songs', *Greece & Rome*, 24/2 (1977), 149–53 (p. 152).

95. Delacour, *Waterfowl*, pp. 197–8.

96. Daniel Giraud Elliot, *The Wild Fowl of the United States and British Possessions* (London: Suckling, 1898), pp. 24–5.

97. Wilmore, *Swans of the World*, p. 129.

98. Arnott, 'Swan Songs', p. 153.

99. Pliny, *Natural History*, tr. Rackham, p. 333 n. 'b'.

2   TRANSFORMATION OF MEN, WOMEN, AND CHILDREN

1. Homer, *Odyssey* XI.298; Apollodorus, *Bibliotheca* III.10; Euripides, *Helen* 16–21; Pindar, *Nemean* X.80–2; all mention the relationship. See Jennifer R. March, 'Leda', in *Dictionary of Classical Mythology* (Oxford: Oxbow Books, 2014), pp. 285–7.

2. Ovid, *Metamorphoses*, VI.109 (pp. 296–7).

3. Ovid, *Metamorphoses*, VIII.301–302 (pp. 426–7). Some discrepancies exist over who fathered which child.

4. Fulgentius, *Mythographi*, in *Auctores Mythographi Latini*, ed. Augustino van Staveren (Lugduni Batavorum: Samuelem Luchtmans, J. Wetstenium, and G. Smith, 1742), II.16 (pp. 694–5);

tr. Leslie George Whitbread (Columbus: Ohio State University Press, 1971), II.13.

5. *Mythographi*, II.16 (p. 694); tr. Whitbread (II.13).

6. Such as Leda and the Swan, 50–100 BC, marble bust, Roman; London, British Museum, Item No. 1973,0302.1.

7. R. W. Medlicott, 'Leda and the Swan – An Analysis of the Theme in Myth and Art', *Australian and New Zealand Journal of Psychiatry*, 4 (1970), 15–23.

8. *Ovide Moralisé: poèm du commencement du quatorzième siècle*, ed. C. de Boer, 3 vols (Amsterdam: Johannes Müller, 1920), vol. 2, VI.814–50 (p. 308, l. 825).

9. *Ovide Moralisé*, VI.832–4 (p. 308). Unless specified, translations are my own.

10. *Ovide Moralisé*, VI.838 (p. 308).

11. *Ovide Moralisé*, VI.840–4 (p. 308).

12. Robert Mills, 'Jesus as Monster', in *The Monstrous Middle Ages*, ed. Bettina Bildhauer and Robert Mills (Cardiff: Wales University Press, 2003), pp. 28–54.

13. For example, Gerald of Wales uses Christ's divine transformation from God to man as proof that God can transform a man into a wolf. See *The History and Topography of Ireland*, tr. John J. O'Meara (London: Penguin, 1982), pp. 69–72.

14. Such as Cycnus son of Ares, in Pausanias (*Description of Greece*, I.27), Euripides (*Heracles*, 390), or Apollodorus (*Bibliotheca*, II.7.7).

15. Ovid, *Metamorphoses*, II.373–7 (pp. 86–7), with slight adjustments.

16. Ovid, *Metamorphoses*, VII.379 (pp. 368–9).

17. Ovid, *Metamorphoses*, XII.144–5 (pp. 190–1).

18. Ovid, *Metamorphoses*, tr. Charles Martin, *Norton Critical Edition* (New York: W. W. Norton & Company, 2010), p. 321 n. 5.

19. *Metamorphoses*, tr. Martin, p. 44 n. 2.

20. *The Middle English Text of Caxton's Ovid, Books II–III, with Parallel Text of The Ovide moralisé en prose II*, ed. Wolfgang Mager (Heidelberg: Universitätsverlag Winter, 2016), pp. 24–9 (p. 27).

21. *Middle English Text of Caxton's Ovid*, p. 27.
22. William Caxton, *The Booke of Ovyde Named Methamorphose*, ed. Richard J. Moll (Oxford: The Bodleian Library, 2013), XII.694–5 (p. 390). See also James G. Clark, Frank T. Coulson, Kathryn L. McKinley (eds), *Ovid in the Middle Ages* (Cambridge: Cambridge University Press, 2011).
23. For birds as human souls, see Godman, *Poetry*, pp. 69–70.
24. A swan also appears in Marie's *Milun* with the swan as messenger between lovers.
25. 'swan-maiden, n.' under 'swan, C4.', OED *Online*, Oxford University Press, December 2021, *www.oed.com/view/Entry/195413* (accessed 21 January 2022).
26. See A. T. Hatto, 'The Swan Maiden: A Folk-tale of North Eurasian Origin?', *Bulletin of the School of Oriental and African Studies*, 24/2 (1961), 326–52; Stith Thompson, *The Folktale* (New York: Holt, Rinehart, and Winston, 1946), pp. 88–93; Kate Watkins Tibbals, 'Elements of Magic in the Romance of William of Palerne', *Modern Philology*, 1 (1904), 355–71; and Tom Peete Cross, 'The Celtic Elements in the Lays of *Lanval* and *Graelent*', *Modern Philology*, 12/10 (1915), 585–644.
27. Thompson, *Folktale*, p. 88.
28. William Henry Schofield, 'The Lays of Graelent and Lanval, and the Story of Wayland', *PMLA*, 15/2 (1900), 121–80.
29. This argument stems from joint research, conducted by myself and Dr. Alex Wilson, currently in preparation.
30. *Völundarkviða*, in *The Poetic Edda: Volume II Mythological Poems*, tr. Ursula Dronke (Oxford: Clarendon Press, 1997), pp. 239–328 (p. 244).
31. *Völundarkviða*, tr. Dronke, p. 255.
32. Alaric Hall, *Elves in Anglo-Saxon England* (Woodbridge: Boydell Press, 2007), pp. 39–47.
33. John McKinnell, 'The Context of *Völundarkviða*', *Saga-Book*, 23 (1990), 1–27 (p. 16).
34. *Friedrich von Schwaben aus der Stuttgarter Handschrift*, ed. Max

Hermann Jellinek (Berlin: Weidmannsche,1904), ll. 4389–61.
See Edwin Bonsack, *Dvalinn: The Relationship of the Friedrich Von Schwaben, Vǫlundarkviða, and Sǫarla Þáttr* (Wiesbaden: Franz Steiner Verlag, 1983), pp. 6–13.

35. *Friedrich*, ll. 4323–5 (p. 66).

36. Schofield, 'Lays', p. 133.

37. *Graelent* in *French Arthurian Literature: IV Eleven Old French Narrative Lays*, ed. and tr. Glyn S. Burgess and Leslie C. Brook (Cambridge: D. S. Brewer, 2007), pp. 349–412 (l. 237, pp. 386–7).

38. *Guingamor*, in *Eleven Old French Narrative Lays*, ed. and tr. Burgess and Brook, pp. 141–95.

39. *Guingamor*, l. 437 (pp. 180–1).

40. Hatto, 'Swan Maiden', pp. 346–8; Schofield, 'Lays', pp. 133–7; Cross, 'Celtic Elements', pp. 616–21.

41. Johannis de Alta Silva, *Dolopathos: Sive de Rege et Septem Sapientibus*, ed. Hermann Oesterley (Strassburg: Karl J. Trübner, 1873), pp. 73–9 (p. 74); Old French by Herbert, *Le Roman de Dolopathos*, ed. Jean-Luc Leclanche, 3 vols (Paris: Honoré Champion, 1997), pp. 351–80. See Henry Alfred Todd, 'La Naissance du Chevalier au Cygne ou les Enfants Changes en Cygnes', *Modern Language Association*, 4/3 (1889), i–xv.

42. *La Naissance du Chevalier au Cygne: Elioxe and Beatrix*, ed. Emanuel J. Mickel, Jr. and Jan A. Nelson, *The Old French Crusade Cycle*, vol. 1 (Tuscaloosa: University of Alabama Press, 1977), l. 261 (p. 7). See also W. R. J. Barron, '*Chevalere Assigne* and the *Naissance du Chevalier au Cygne*', *Medium Ævum*, 36/1 (1967), 25–37; and 'Versions and Texts of the *Naissance du Chevalier au Cygne*', *Romania*, 89 (1968), 481–538.

43. *La Naissance, Elioxe*, l. 1635 (p. 37).

44. *La Naissance, Beatrix*, ll. 63–8 (p. 132).

45. *La Naissance, Beatrix*, ll. 77–8 (p. 132).

46. See Eugene O'Curry, 'The *Trí thruaighe na scéalaigheachta* of Erinn: II *The Fate of the Children of Lir*', *Atlantis*, 4 (1863), 113–57.

47. Cross, 'Celtic Elements', pp. 36–7; *Völundarkviða*, tr. Dronke, pp. 258–9.

48. Cross, 'Celtic Elements', pp. 620–1.

49. *Völundarkviða*, ed. and tr. Dronke, pp. 243–4.

50. Catharina Raudvere, *Witchcraft and Magic in Europe: The Middle Ages* (London: Athlone Press, 2002), pp. 101–7.

51. *Völundarkviða*, ed. and tr. Dronke, p. 301.

52. Thompson, *Folktale*, p. 88.

53. *Children of Lir*, tr. O'Curry, pp. 113–57.

54. For textual relationship, see Anthony R. Wagner, 'The Swan Badge and the Swan Knight', *Archaeologia*, 97 (1959), 127–38.

55. This scene is depicted on a casket, fifteenth century, bone carving, Italian. London, British Museum, Item No. 1885, 0804.13.

56. *Dolopathos*, p. 79; translation mine. See also *Dolopathos*, tr. Brady B. Gilleland (Binghamton: State University of New York, 1981), pp. 71–7.

57. *La Naissance*, ed. Mickel and Nelson, p. lxxxxiii.

58. *La Naissance, Elioxe*, ll. 3373–6 (p. 74).

59. *La Naissance, Elioxe*, ll. 3483–4 (p. 76).

60. *La Naissance, Beatrix*, l. 2556 (p. 187). See also Peggy McCracken, *In the Skin of a Beast: Sovereignty and Animality in Medieval France* (Chicago: Chicago University Press, 2017), pp. 131–8.

61. *La Naissance*, ed. Mickel and Nelson, p. lxxxxvii.

62. Tony Davenport, 'Abbreviation and the Education of the Hero in *Chevalere Assigne*', in *The Matter of Identity in Medieval Romance*, ed. Phillipa Hardman (Cambridge: D. S. Brewer, 2002), pp. 9–20.

63. *Chevelere Assigne*, in *Medieval English Romances*, ed. Diane Speed, 2 vols (Durham: Durham Medieval Texts, 1993), pp. 149–70 (ll. 359–61, p. 169).

64. *La Fin d'Elias*, lines 703–8 (p. 376), tr. McCracken, *Skin of a Beast*, p. 137.

65. Robert Copland, *The History of Helyas, Knight of the Swan* (London: William Pickering, 1827), p. 112.

66. See Timothy McFarland, 'The Emergence of the German Grail Romance', in W. H. Jackson and S. A. Ranawake (eds), *The Arthur of the Germans: The Arthurian Legend in Medieval German and Dutch Literature* (Cardiff: University of Wales Press, 2000), pp. 54–68. For the Swan Knight Saga, see Claude Lecouteux, 'Zur Entstehung der Schwanrittersage', *Zeitschrift für deutsches Altertum und deutsche Literatur*, 107 (1978), 18–33; and Robert Jaffray, *The Two Knights of the Swan, Lohengrin and Helyas* (New York: G. P. Putnam's Sons, 1910).

67. Wolfram von Eschenbach, *Parzival*, ed. Joachim Bumke (Tübingen: Max Niemeyer, 2008), XVI.24664–66 (pp. 728–9); tr. A. T. Hatto (London: Penguin, 1980), p. 409.

68. For a detailed study to which I am much indebted, see Alastair Matthews, *The Medieval German Lohengrin: Narrative Poetics in the Story of the Swan Knight* (Rochester, NY: Camden House, 2016), especially pp. 81–4 and 92–6. Quotations and translations to *Lohengrin* follow Matthews, from *Lohengrin: Edition und Untersuchungen*, ed. Thomas Cramer (Munich: Fink, 1971).

69. See Matthews, *Lohengrin: Narrative Poetics*, p. 82–3.

70. *Lohengrin*, 78.771–7, following Matthews, *Lohengrin: Narrative Poetics*, pp. 83–4.

71. *Lohengrin*, 532.5317–9, following Matthews, *Lohengrin: Narrative Poetics*, p. 93.

72. *Lohengrin*, 700.6991–3, following Matthews, *Lohengrin: Narrative Poetics*, p. 117.

73. W. H. Jackson, 'Lorengel and the Spruch von den Tafelrundern', in Jackson and Ranawake (eds), *The Arthur of the Germans*, pp. 181–3 (p. 181).

74. Lecouteux, 'Schwanenrittersage', pp. 18–33; Alastair Matthews, 'When is the Swan Knight Not the Swan Knight? Berthold von Holle's *Demantin* and Literary Space in Medieval Europe', *Modern Language Review*, 112/3 (2017), 666–85.

75. *The Continuations of the Old French Perceval of Chretien de Troyes*, ed. William Roach, 5 vols (Philadelphia: American Philosophical

Society, 1952), vol. 3, pt. 1, ll. 8352–68, Branch VI, MS L (p. 530).
See Keith Busby, 'The Continuations', in Glyn S. Burgess and
Karen Pratt (eds), *The Arthur of the French: The Arthurian Legend in
Medieval French and Occitan Literature* (Cardiff: University of Wales
Press, 2006), pp. 222–47.

3 THE DESCENDANTS OF THE SWAN KNIGHT

1. Bitterli, *Say What*, p. 39.
2. See William Yarrell, *A History of British Birds*, vol. 4 (London:
   John van Voorst, 1884–5), p. 327.
3. Francis Klingender, *Animals in Art and Thought to the End of the
   Middle Ages* (London: Routledge & Kegan Paul, 1971), pp. 114–19.
4. Gerald of Wales, *The Life of St. Hugh of Avalon, Bishop of Lincoln
   1186–1200*, tr. Richard M. Loomis (New York: Garland Publishing,
   1985), Ch. X, pp. 32–5 (pp. 32–3).
5. Adam of Eynsham, *Magna Vita Sancti Hugonis. The Life of St Hugh
   of Lincoln*, tr. Decima L. Douie and David Hugh Farmer, 2 vols
   (Oxford: Clarendon Press, 1985), pp. 103–9 (p. 105).
6. The inscription reads 'OR LOONS: DIEU' (Now let us praise
   God). It is possibly of French origin. See Hugh Tait, 'Pilgrim-
   Signs and Thomas, Earl of Lancaster', *British Museum Quarterly*, 20
   (1955), 39–47.
7. See Simon John, 'Godfrey of Bouillon and the Swan Knight', in
   Simon John and Nicholas Morton (eds), *Crusading and Warfare in
   the Middle Ages* (London: Routledge, 2014), pp. 129–42, to which
   I am indebted. I have chosen the traditional rendering of
   'Godfrey of Bouillon', rather than 'Godfrey of Boulogne'.
   Throughout the text I have opted for this spelling of 'Bouillon',
   but I refer to the northern county in France, whose city is known
   today as 'Boulogne' or 'Boulogne-sur-Mer'.
8. Albert of Aachen, *Historia Ierosolimitana: History of the Journey to
   Jerusalem*, ed. and tr. Susan B. Edgington (Oxford: Clarendon
   Press, 2007).

9. Laura Hibbard Loomis, *Mediæval Romance in England* (New York: Burt Franklin, 1969), pp. 239–62 (p. 249); John, 'Godfrey [...] and The Swan Knight', p. 132, from *Liber Epistolarum Guidonis de Basochis*, ed. Herbert Adolfsson (Stockholm, 1969), p. 95.

10. Geoffrey of Clairvaux (Geoffrey of Auxerre), *Commento alla Apoccalisse*, Serm XV and Hélinand of Froidmont, *Chronicorum liber* IV, following Ferruccio Gastaldelli, 'Una Sconosciuta Redazione Latina della *Chanson du Chevalier au Cygne* nel *Commento All'Apocalisse* di Goffredo d'Auxerre', *Aevum*, 42 (1968), pp. 491–501.

11. William of Tyre, *Chronicon*, ed. R. B. C. Huygens (Turnholt: Brepols, 1986), IX, vi (p. 427); William of Tyre, A *History of Deeds Done Beyond the Sea*, tr. Emily Atwater Babcock and A. C. Krey, 2 vols (New York: Columbia University Press, 1943), IX.6 (p.388).

12. *La Chanson d'Antioche*, ed. Suzanne Duparc-Quioc, 2 vols (Paris: Paul Geuthner, 1977), ll. 7453, 7472–3 (pp. 372–3); tr. Susan B. Edgington and Carol Sweetenham (Farnham: Ashgate, 2011), p. 277. See also Maurice Keen, *Chivalry* (New Haven: Yale University Press, 1984), pp. 57–9; Simon John, "Li bons dus de buillon': Genre Conventions and the Depiction of Godfrey of Bouillon in the *Chanson d'Antioche* and the *Chanson de Jérusalem*', in Andrew D. Buck and Thomas W. Smith (eds), *Remembering the Crusades in Medieval Texts and Songs* (Cardiff: University of Wales Press, 2019), pp. 83–100.

13. *La Conquête de Jérusalem*, ed. Célestin Hippeau (Paris: A. Aubry, 1868), ll. 7241–2 (p. 285); tr. John, 'Godfrey [...] and the Swan Knight', p. 134.

14. *Conquête de Jérusalem*, ll. 7761–3 (p. 307); tr. John, 'Godfrey [...] and the Swan Knight', p. 134.

15. The Volumes of *The Old French Crusade Cycle* (Tuscaloosa: University of Alabama Press) include: Volume I: *La Naissance du Chevalier au Cygne*, ed. Mickel and Nelson (1977); Volume II: *Le Chevalier au Cygne and La Fin d'Elias*, ed. Jan A. Nelson (1985);

and Volume III: *Les Enfances Godefroi and Le Retour de Cornumarant*, ed. Emanuel J. Mickel (1999).

16. The legendary Swan Knight was one famous medieval ancestor among many. Melusine was another. See Susan Crane, *The Performance of Self: Ritual, Clothing, and Identity During the Hundred Years War* (Philadelphia: University of Pennsylvania Press, 2002), pp. 107–25.

17. Wagner, 'Swan Badge', pp. 127–38.

18. *Parzival*, tr. Hatto, notes p. 409.

19. Konrad von Würzburg, *Der Schwanritter*, ed. Franz Roth (Frankfurt am Main: C. Naumann, 1861), ll. 1320–3 (p. 37).

20. Jaffray, *Two Knights*, pp. 83–94.

21. Wagner, 'Swan Badge', p. 132.

22. *Mémoires d'Olivier de la Marche*, ed. Henri Beaune et J. d'Arbaumont (Paris: Henri Loones, 1884), tome ii, p. 341; tr. Wagner, 'Swan Badge', p. 132, with minor adjustments. Olivier also records Melusine featuring in the décor at the Feast of the Swan (see endnote 8 of this chapter).

23. John, 'Godfrey [...] and The Swan Knight', p. 140.

24. John, 'Godfrey [...] and The Swan Knight', p. 140, following Jacob of Maerlant, *Spiegel Historiael*, ed. Matthias de Vries and Eelco Verwijs Verwijs, 3 vols (Leiden, 1863–79), vol. 3., p. 318.

25. D'Arcy Jonathan Dacre Boulton, *The Knights of the Crown: The Monarchical Orders of Knighthood in Later Medieval Europe, 1325–1520* (Woodbridge: Boydell Press, 2000), p. 486.

26. Boulton, *Knights of the Crown*, p. 397; Conversely, Keen states this was founded by Duke Albert Achilles of Brandenberg in 1444 (*Chivalry*, p. 179). On chivalric orders, see Keen, *Chivalry*, pp. 179–99; Malcolm Vale, *War and Chivalry* (London: Duckworth, 1981), pp. 33–62.

27. Keen, *Chivalry*, p. 182.

28. Boulton, *Knights of the Crown*, pp. 397 n. 2. Three sketches of the collar appear on p. 592.

29. Boulton, *Knights of the Crown*, pp. 642–3.

30. Boulton, *Knights of the Crown*, pp. 249–51 (p. 251). It is likely this order disbanded several years after its creation.

31. Erich Juethe, *Der Minnesänger Hiltbolt von Schwangau* (Hildesheim: Georg Olms Verlag, 1977).

32. Raymond Cazelles and Johannes Rathofer, *Illuminations of Heaven and Earth: The Glories of the Très Riches Heures du Duc de Berry* (New York: Harry N. Abrams, 1988), p. 72; Michel Pastoureau, *Les signes et les songes: Études sur la symbolique et la sensibilité médiévales* (Florence: Sismel-Edizioni del Galluzzo, 2013), pp. 87–110. John also employed the bear ('ursine') as his symbol, which may also be related to his use of the swan. The bear may be a word-play on the name of one of his favourites, called Ursine, thus our+cygne (our swan).

33. Roger A. D'Hulst, *Flemish Tapestries from the Fifteenth to the Eighteenth Century* (Brussels: Editions Arcade, 1967), p. 75.

34. Joseph Calmette, *The Golden Age of Burgundy: The Magnificent Dukes and their Courts*, tr. Doreen Weightman (London: Weidenfeld and Nicolson, 1962), p. 69. A swan-badge was also used by the most famous pedophile and serial killer of the Middle Ages, Gilles de Rais (d. 1400), a French knight.

35. The Swan Knight Tapestries exist now in only two fragments: one at the Wawel Royal Castle in Krakow, previously held, I believe, at the Church of St Catherine in the same city; and one, damaged by fire, in Oesterreichisches Museum für angewandte Kunst in Vienna. See also D'Hulst, *Flemish Tapestries*, pp. 58, 75.

36. Richard Vaughan, *Philip the Good: The Apogee of Burgundy* (Woodbridge: Boydell Press, 1970), p. 152.

37. Calmette, *Golden Age*, p. 134.

38. Calmette, *Golden Age*, p. 138.

39. *The Red Book of the Exchequer: Volume 2*, ed. Hubert Hall (Cambridge: Cambridge University Press, 2012), pp. 753–4.

40. Wagner, 'Swan Badge'. See also Laurent Hablot, 'Embèmatique et mythologie médiévale, le cygne, une devise princière', *Histoire de l'art*, 49 (2001), 51–64. I have opted for the spelling of 'Tony' rather than 'de Tony', and 'Bohun', rather than 'de Bohun'.

41. Constance Bullock-Davies, *Menestrellorum Multitudo: Minstrels at a Royal Feast* (Cardiff: University of Wales Press, 1978), p. xv.

42. Constance Bullock-Davies, *Menestrellorum*, p. xxx with minor adjustments, from *Flores Historiarum*, ed. Luad (RS), III, 131–2.

43. Keen, *Chivalry*, pp. 213–15, 276 n. 60.

44. Matthew Ward, *The Livery Collar in Late Medieval England and Wales* (Woodbridge: Boydell Press, 2016), p. 59.

45. Lucia Diaz Pascual, 'The Heraldry of the de Bohun Earls', *The Antiquaries Journal*, 100 (2020), 1–24 (p. 13), from The National Archives (TNA), Public Record Office (PRO), DL 27/14.

46. Pascual, 'Bohun Earls', p. 13.

47. Pascual, 'Bohun Earls', p. 13, from TNA, PRO, DL 25/29.

48. *Chevelere Assigne*, l. 270 (p. 167).

49. Pascual, 'Bohun Earls', pp. 4, 6, 14.

50. Pascual, 'Bohun Earls', p. 13.

51. John A. Goodall, 'Heraldry in the Decoration of English Medieval Manuscripts', *The Antiquaries Journal*, 77 (1997), 179–220 (p. 213); Janet Backhouse, *Medieval Birds in the Sherborne Missal* (London: British Library, 2001).

52. Juliet Vale, *Edward III and Chivalry: Chivalric Society and Its Context 1270–1350* (Woodbridge: Boydell Press, 1982), pp. 69, 175, from London, PRO, E372/207 m. 50; E101/391/15.

53. Vale, *Edward III*, p. 175, from London, PRO, E372/207 m. 50; E101/391/15.

54. Jenny Stratford, *Richard II and the English Royal Treasure* (Woodbridge: Boydell Press, 2012), p. 50.

55. For swans used by Edward I, Edward III, the Black Prince, Richard II, John of Gaunt, Humphrey de Bohun, Thomas of Woodstock, Henry IV, Henry V, and more, see Michael Powell

Siddons, *Heraldic Badges in England and Wales: Volume* II, Part 1, *Royal Badges* (Woodbridge: Boydell Press, 2009), pp. 239–45.

56. Siddons, *Heraldic Badges*, Plate 43.

57. 'Eleanor de Bohun, Duchess of Gloucester', Westminster Abbey, *https://www.westminster-abbey.org/abbey-commemorations/commemorations/eleanor-de-bohun-duchess-of-gloucester.*

58. Chris Given-Wilson, 'Richard II and the Higher Nobility', in Anthony Goodman and James Gillespie (eds), *Richard* II: *The Art of Kingship* (Oxford: Clarendon Press, 1999), pp. 107–28 (pp. 110–12).

59. R 470, R 1034, and R 18, in Stratford, *Royal Treasure*, pp. 188, 240, 147, 80, 266.

60. R 126 and R 880 in Stratford, *Royal Treasure*, pp. 80, 158, 224, 280, 332.

61. Stratford, *Royal Treasure*, pp. 189, 306.

62. Richard Marks and Paul Williamson (eds), *Gothic Art for England 1400–1547* (London: V&A Publications, 2003), pp. 204, 326–8; John Cherry, 'The Dunstable Swan Jewel', *Journal of the British Archaeological Association*, 32/1 (1969), 38–53.

63. Stratford, *Royal Treasure*, pp. 58–9. Scot McKendrick, 'Tapestries from the Low Countries in England during the Fifteenth Century', in Caroline Barron and Nigel Saul (eds), *England and the Low Countries in the Late Middles Ages* (New York: St Martin's Press, 1995), pp. 43–60 (p. 45 and nn. 15 and 16).

64. Given-Wilson, 'Higher Nobility', p. 123.

65. Arthur Charles Fox-Davies, A *Complete Guide to Heraldry* (London: Thomas Nelson and Sons, 1950), pp. 245, 453–70.

66. Michael Bennett, 'Gower, Richard II, and Henry IV', in Stephen H. Rigby and Siân Echard (eds), *Historians on John Gower* (Cambridge: D. S. Brewer, 2019), pp. 209–42 (p. 220).

67. Martha Carlin, 'Gower's Life', in Rigby and Echard (eds), *Historians on John Gower*, pp. 32–85 (pp. 68–78).

68. Marks and Williamson (eds), *Gothic Art*, pp. 204–5. See also Swan Livery Badge, London, British Museum, England fifteenth century, lead alloy, Item No. 1904,0720.19.

69. Given-Wilson, 'Higher Nobility', p. 124.
70. Given-Wilson, 'Higher Nobility', p. 126; Chris Given-Wilson, *The Royal Household and the King's Affinity: Service, Politics and Finance in England* 1360–1413 (London: Yale University Press, 1986), pp. 236–42.
71. Given-Wilson, 'Higher Nobility', p. 126; Given-Wilson, *Royal Household*, pp. 236–42; *Historia Vitae et Regni Ricardi Secundi*, ed. George B. Stow (Philadelphia: University of Pennsylvania Press, 1977), p. 132.
72. her = their; 'On the Deposition of Richard II', in Thomas Wright (ed.), *Political Poems and Songs Relating to English History*, vol. 1 (London: Longman, Green, Longman, & Roberts, 1859), pp. 368–417 (p. 381).
73. Given-Wilson, 'Higher Nobility', p. 126.
74. A. J. Pollard, *Late Medieval England, 1399–1509* (Harlow: Pearson Education, 2000), pp. 19–25.
75. 'On King Richard's Ministers, 1399' in *Political Poems*, ed. Wright, pp. 363–6, sts. 3, 6, and p. 363 n. 5.
76. Bennett, 'Gower, Richard II', in Rigby and Echard (eds), *Historians on John Gower*, p. 232.
77. John Gower, *Poems on Contemporary Events: the* Visio Anglie (1381) *and* Cronica tripertita (1400), ed. David R. Carlson, tr. A. G. Rigg (Toronto: Pontifical Institute of Mediaeval Studies, 2011), CT III.368–71 (pp. 320–1).
78. J. R. Planche, 'On the Badges of the House of Lancaster', *Journal of the British Archaeological Association*, 6/4 (1851), 374–93.
79. Goodall, 'Heraldry', p. 210.
80. Ward, *Livery Collar*, p. 57.
81. W. H. St John Hope, 'IV. The Funeral, Monument, and Chantry Chapel of King Henry the Fifth', *Archaeologia*, 65 (1914), 128–86 (pp. 143–4).
82. John Cherry, 'The Dunstable Swan Jewel', in Marks and Williamson (eds), *Gothic Art*, p. 205.

83. Wagner, 'Swan Badge', Plate XL.

84. John Rous, *The Rous Roll*, ed. Charles Ross (Gloucester: Alan Sutton, 1980), No. 18. All quotations follow this edition.

85. Rous, *Rous Roll*, No. 18.

86. Rous, *Rous Roll*, No. 18.

87. Copland, *Helyas*, p. 2.

88. Pollard, *Medieval England*, pp. 282–6.

89. Pollard, *Medieval England*, pp. 334–7.

4 COOKERY, HUSBANDRY AND THE LAW

1. Following Henry III, 1247–51, Close Rolls, 35 Henry III, 1251, m. 1 (pp. 521–2).

2. Miranda Threlfall-Holmes, *Monks and Markets: Durham Cathedral Priory* 1460–1520 (Oxford: Oxford University Press, 2005), p. 47, from DCM Bursar/cellarer indentures, 1504/5.

3. Peter Brears, *Cooking and Dining in Medieval England* (Totnes: Prospect Books, 2008), p. 468.

4. *Durham Priory Manorial Accounts, 1277–1310*, ed. Richard Britnell (Woodbridge: Boydell Press, 2014), p. 133. Futures references shortened to DPMA.

5. Following Henry III, 1247–51, Close Rolls, 35 Henry III, 1251, m. 1 (pp. 521–2).

6. Bullock-Davies, *Menestrellorum*, p. xxviii.

7. Bullock-Davies, *Menestrellorum*, p. xxix.

8. *Curye on Inglysch: English Culinary Manuscripts of the Fourteenth Century*, ed. Constance B. Hieatt and Sharon Butler (Oxford: Oxford University Press, 1985), pp. 2–3; and Terence Scully, *The Art of Cookery in the Middle Ages* (Woodbridge: Boydell Press, 1995), pp. 120–1.

9. Brears, *Cooking and Dining*, pp. 379, 472–3.

10. Master Chiquart, *De fait de cuisine / On Cookery of Master Chiquart* (1420), tr. Terence Scully (Tempe: Arizona Center for Medieval and Renaissance Studies, 2010), pp. 139–40.

11. Chiquart, *On Cookery*, p. 127.

12. Scully, *Art of Cookery*, p. 162.

13. Chiquart, *On Cookery*, p. 139 n. 10.10.

14. Joop Witteveen, 'On Swans, Cranes, and Herons: Part 1, Swans', *Petits Propos Culinaires*, 24 (1986), 22–31 (p. 25).

15. The instructions are for a chicken but extend to any fowl: 'preng ung poullet ou aultre oisel tel qu'il te plaira' (get a chicken or any other bird you want), Recipe 58 (p. 81) from *The Vivendier: A Fifteenth-Century French Cookery Manuscript*, tr. Terence Scully (Totnes: Prospect Books, 1997).

16. Witteveen, 'On Swans', p. 26.

17. Witteveen, 'On Swans', p. 26.

18. The following quotations are from *A Noble Boke off Cookry ffor a Prynce Houssolde*, ed. Robina Napier (London: Elliot Stock, 1882), pp. 4–5; tr. Brears, *Cooking and Dining*, p. 359, slightly modified.

19. *Curye*, p. 85.

20. *Curye*, p. 131.

21. Brears, *Cooking and Dining*, p. 227.

22. *Carmina Burana*, ed. Peter Diemer, Dorothee Diemer, Benedikt Konrad Vollman (Berlin: Deutscher Klassiker Verlag, 2016), Song 130 (p. 460); tr. David Parlett, in *Selections from the Carmina Burana* (Middlesex: Penguin, 1986), pp. 130–1 (CB130), with minor adjustments.

23. The following paragraph follows Norman F. Ticehurst, *The Mute Swan in England* (London: Cleaver-Hume Press, 1957), p. 15. Twelve pence equal one shilling.

24. From *Extracts from the Municipal Records of the City of York during the Reigns of Edward IV, Edward V, and Richard II*, ed. Robert Davies (London: J. B. Nichols and Son, 1843), p. 55, with expanded abbreviations.

25. DPMA 1277–1310, p. 25.

26. DPMA 1277–1310, p. 103.

27. Ticehurst, *Mute Swan*, p. 13, following *Records of Lydd*, p. 94.

28. Ticehurst, *Mute Swan*, p. 75.

29. Kent History and Library Centre (KHLC): Probate Court Records (PCR), 32/4, fol. 189; KHLC: PRC 32/9, fol. 75; KHLC: PRC 32/24, fol. 9; and KHLC: PRC 32nd /28, fol. 76.

30. DPMA 1277–1310, p. 262.

31. DPMA 1277–1310, pp. 142, 262, 302.

32. Arthur MacGregor, 'Swan Rolls and Beak Markings: Husbandry, Exploitation and Regulation of *Cygnus olor* in England, *c.*1100–1900', *Anthropozoologica*, 22 (1996), 39–68 (pp. 62–3).

33. Such activities are featured in the Devonshire Hunting Tapestries: *The Bear, Otter, and Swan Hunt*, at the Victoria and Albert Museum. See D'Hulst, *Flemish Tapestries*, pp. 41–8.

34. Witteveen, 'On Swans', p. 24. We know that Swan Marking occurred on the Continent by the reign of Charles V (1500–58). As Holy Roman Emperor, he was ruler over Northern Germany, the Low Countries, Austria, Spain, and parts of France and Italy.

35. MacGregor, 'Swan Rolls', p. 49.

36. MacGregor, 'Swan Rolls', pp. 51–2.

37. MacGregor, 'Swan Rolls', p. 52.

38. Oxford, Bodleian Library, Ms. Bodley 204, fol. 124b^v, *c.*1340, featured in Ticehurst, *Mute Swan*, Plate XI (a); MacGregor, 'Swan Rolls', p. 53.

39. Ticehurst, *Mute Swan*, p. 90.

40. Ticehurst, *Mute Swan*, p. 91.

41. Edward I, 1272–1281, Cal. Pat. Rolls, 4 Ed. I, Nov. 1276, m. 3d (p. 183).

42. 1482 *Rolls of Parl.* VI. 224/1, following 'swanherd', OED *Online*, Oxford University Press, March 2021, *www.oed.com/view/Entry/*195420 (accessed 1 May 2021).

43. Edward II, 1313–1317, Cal. Pat. Rolls, 8 Ed. II, pt. 1, Oct. 1314, m. 14d (p. 244).

44. Edward III, 1364–1367, Cal. Pat. Rolls, 39 Ed. III, pt. 1, Feb. 1365, m. 26d (p. 142).

Plate 1: *Swans singing to human lyre, 1309– c.1325.Oxford, Bodleian Library, MS Douce 308, fol. 88v. © Bodleian Libraries, University of Oxford. CC-BY-NC 4.0.*

Plate 2: *The Knight of the Swan (left) pulled by his ducally-gorged swan-brother; his mother (right) in bedrest after giving birth to septuplets, the seven swan-children, including the future Swan Knight, c.1444–5. London, British Library, Talbot Shrewsbury Book, MS Royal 15 E VI, fol. 273r. © British Library Board.*

Plate 3 (above): *Swan Knight Tapestry, fifteenth century, from Flanders. Krakow, Wawel Royal Castle. Photograph: Adam Wierzba © Wawel Royal Castle. Young Enyas (the future Swan Knight) feeds his siblings who have been transformed into swans.*

Plate 4 (opposite): *Saint Hugh of Lincoln, 1490–1500, altarpiece from Thuison-les-Abbeville, Picardy, France. Chicago, Art Institute of Chicago, 1933.1060. CC0. Public domain. The swan is chained, like the Bohun swan, and noses up the Bishop's sleeve as his does in Hugh's* Vita.

Plate 5 (opposite, top): *Chronicle of the Princes of Clèves, 1401–1500. Paris, Bibliothèque Nationale de France, de France, MS Français 5607, fol. 1r. Public domain. Beatrice of Clèves in her swan tower, with the Swan Knight as he departs.*

Plate 6 (opposite, bottom): *Hiltbolt von Schwangao, the Poet Minstrel, featuring black swan headpiece, c.1300–c.1340. Heidelberg, Universitätsbibliothek, Cod. Pal. germ. 848, Große Heidelberger Liederhandschrift (Codex Manesse); 146r.*

Plate 7 (below): *Two Bohun swans ducally gorged in arms of Peter de Courtenay, Bishop of Exeter Cathedral, fifteenth century, chimney piece. Exeter, Exeter Cathedral. Public domain.*

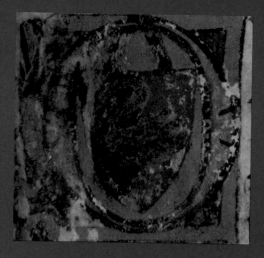

Plate 8 (left): *Swan badge on field of red and black, in the livery colours of Thomas Woodstock, c.1385–99.* San Marino, California, The Huntington Library, shield on Huntington MS EL 26 A 17, fol. 1r. Public domain. *Compare with Figure 14.*

Plate 9: *Dunstable Jewel, c.1400, white enamel, England.* London, British Museum, Item No: 1966,0703.1. © *The Trustees of the British Museum. This white jewel resembles the Bohun Swan and was likely a livery badge during the reign of Richard II, possibly employed by Henry Bolingbroke or Thomas of Woodstock. Compare with Plate 10.*

Plate 10: The White Hart of Richard II, Wilton Diptych, c.1395–9.
London, the National Gallery. © The National Gallery, London.
Richard II's White Hart is almost a perfect foil to the badge of
the Bohun Swan employed by Richard II's adversaries (displayed
across in the Dunstable Jewel). Both are white, ducally gorged,
and intimately associated with royalty.

Plate 11: *Her majesty attends the Swan Uppings c.2019, the first known English monarch to do so.* PA Images / Alamy Stock Photo.

45. Ticehurst, *Mute Swan*, p. 19.
46. Edward I, 1272–1281, Cal. Pat. Rolls, 4 Ed. I, Nov. 1276, m. 3d (p. 183).
47. Edward III, 1354–1358, Cal. Pat. Rolls, 29 Ed. III, pt. III, m. 12 (p. 308).
48. Edward III, 1361–1364, Cal. Pat. Rolls, 35 Ed III, pt. II, m. 27 (p. 15).
49. Ticehurst, *Mute Swan*, p. 54.
50. Ticehurst, *Mute Swan*, p. 58.
51. Edward IV 1461–67, Cal. Pat. Rolls, 3 Ed. IV, pt. I, m. 17d.
52. Ticehurst, *Mute Swan*, pp. 19–20, from *Act for Swans*, 1482, 22. Ed. IV, c. 6.
53. Edward IV, *Act for Swans* (1482).
54. Ticehurst, *Mute Swan*, p. 39.
55. Ticehurst, *Mute Swan*, p. 39.
56. Ticehurst, *Mute Swan*, pp. 39–40. To be 'in mercy' means to be liable to amercement, ie a random fine at the discretion of the court.
57. Ticehurst, *Mute Swan*, pp. 39–53.
58. Ticehurst, *Mute Swan*, p. 41, from *Duchy State Papers*, 311.
59. *Act for Swans*, 1482, 22 Ed. IV, c. 6.
60. *Order for Swannes, England and Wales* (London: Henrie Denham, 1584); and Ticehurst, *Mute Swan*, p. 28.
61. James I, *The Order for Swannes both by the Statutes, and by the Auncient Orders and Customes vsed within the Realme of England* (London: *c.*1615–20).
62. *On the Orders, Laws and Ancient Customes of Swanns* (London: August Mathewes, 1632). See also Ticehurst, *Mute Swan*, pp. 32–6.
63. Charles I, *On the Orders of Swanns* (1632).
64. Charles I, *On the Orders of Swanns* (1632).
65. Ticehurst, *Mute Swan*, p. 65.
66. Ticehurst, *Mute Swan*, p. 67, from Hatfield muniments, Cecil paper 203/77.
67. MacGregor, 'Swan Rolls', p. 63.
68. Ticehurst, *Mute Swan*, p. 94.

5   THE AFTERLIVES OF THE MEDIEVAL SWAN

1.   Shakespeare, *Merchant of Venice*, III.ii, and *Othello*, V.ii; Tennyson, 'Dying Swan' (1830); and Coleridge, 'On Volunteer Singers' (1847).

2.   'swansong, n.', OED *Online*, Oxford University Press, December 2021, *www.oed.com/view/Entry/92514881* (accessed 21 January 2022).

3.   Medlicott, 'Leda and the Swan', pp. 15–23.

4.   Sam Parker, 'Police Force Gallery to Remove Leda and the Swan Image for 'Condoning Bestiality', *Huffington Post* UK, 30 April 2012, *https://www.huffingtonpost.co.uk/2012/04/30/gallery-swan-image-condones-bestiality_n_1463675.html*.

5.   'The Six Swans', in *Grimm's Fairy Tales*, tr. Margaret Hunt, ed. Josef Scharl (London: Routledge and Kegan Paul, 1959), pp. 238–43.

6.   Carl Orff, *Carmina Burana: Cantiones profanae* (Mainz: B. Schott's Söhne, 1956), pp. 68–9.

7.   Ross W. Duffin (ed.), A *Performer's Guide to Medieval Music* (Bloomington: Indiana University Press, 2000), pp. 269–70.

8.   Ben Jonson, 'To the Memory of my Beloved Master William Shakespeare', in *The Poetical Works of William Shakespeare and Ben Jonson* (Boston: Houghton Mifflin, 1880), pp. 323–8.

9.   Birkhead and Perrins, *Mute Swan*, pp. 121–40.

10.   For more information on the role of the Crown, the Vintners' Company, and the Dyers' Company in Swan Upping, see their respective websites: *http://www.royalswan.co.uk/*; *https://www.vintnershall.co.uk*; and *https://www.dyerscompany.co.uk*.

11.   'Florida Sells City Swans after Queen's Gift Leads to Overpopulation', BBC, 18 October 2020: *https://www.bbc.co.uk/news/world-us-canada-54572788*.

12.   Barry Millington (ed.), *The Wagner Compendium: A Guide to Wagner's Life and Music* (London: Thames and Hudson, 1992), pp. 282–5.

13.   Julius Desing, *The Royal Castle of Neuschwanstein*, tr. Bonny Schmid-Burleson (Lechbruck: Wilhelm Kienberger, 1998), pp. 5, 66.

14. 'Idea and History: Swan Knight', Schloss Neuschwanstein, Bayerische Schlösserverwaltung, *https://www.neuschwanstein.de/ englisch/idea/schwan.htm* (accessed 22 January 22).

15. *Ludwig II, Letter to Richard Wagner, May 1868, German and English following, https://www.neuschwanstein.de/englisch/idea/index.htm.* See Manfred Eger, 'The Patronage of King Ludwig II', tr. John Deathridge, in Ulrich Müller, Peter Wapnewski (eds), *Wagner Handbook* (Cambridge, MA: Harvard University Press, 1992), pp. 317–26.

16. The follower refers to Desing, *Neuschwanstein*, pp. 13, 26–7, 29, 38–9, 40–1, 45.

17. Desing, *Neuschwanstein*, p. 38.

18. These few references to the great German tradition of the Swan Knight could be the subject of many PhD theses. Much German material has been written on the Swan Knight tradition although some of this is now slightly dated. For excellent starting point, see bibliography of Matthews, *Lohengrin: Narrative Poetics*, pp. 207–30.

19. Walter Crane, *An Artist's Reminiscences* (London: Methuen, 1907), p. 424. See also Thomas Sloane, 'Crane, Walter', in *The Arthurian Encyclopedia*, ed. Norris Lacy (Woodbridge: Boydell Press, 1986), p. 123.

20. J. R. R. Tolkien, *The Return of the King* (New York: Ballantine Books, 1965), p. 50.

21. Tolkien, *Return*, p. 114.

22. Tolkien, *Return*, p. 151–2.

23. Tolkien, *Return*, p. 206.

24. According to Colin Blowbol's *Testament*, following Rowland, *Human Souls*, p. 173.

25. Rowland, *Human Souls*, p. 173.

26. Christopher Lowe, 'The Most Popular Pub Names in 2019', in *The Morning Advertiser*, 22 May 2019, *https://www.morningadvertiser.co.uk/ Article/2019/05/22/What-are-the-most-popular-pub-names-in-the-*UK.

FURTHER READING

Michel Pastoureau, *Les signes et les songes: Études sur la symbolique et la sensibilité médiévales* (Florence: Sismel-Edizioni del Galluzzo, 2013), pp. 87–110: ranging from Godfrey of Bouillon to the English Court, Pastoreau's article covers a variety of swan usages over a long chronology. A great big-picture overview.

Jaffray, Robert, *The Two Knights of the Swan, Lohengrin and Helyas* (New York: G. P. Putnam's Sons, 1910): the place to begin for the Swan Knight's origin, differing legends, and cultural development across medieval vernaculars.

Rowland, Beryl, *Birds with Human Souls: A Guide to Bird Symbolism* (Knoxville: University of Tennessee Press, 1978): a fabulous, dense mine of primary data on medieval swans over a variety of usages. The bibliography is a little difficult to unpack, so I have endeavoured to give a few of those references in this work.

Ticehurst, Norman F., *The Mute Swan in England* (London: Cleaver-Hume Press, 1957): the place to begin for history of swans in England, covering swan laws, swanherds, swan motes, and swan rolls, with hundreds of examples from manuscripts and wonderful images. The eighteen-volume Ticehurst Collection is housed in the Society of Antiquaries, London.

Matthews, Alastair, *The Medieval German Lohengrin: Narrative Poetics in the Story of the Swan Knight* (Rochester, NY: Camden House, 2016): the place to begin when examining the German literary tradition of the Swan Knight, with extensive analysis on the Middle High German *Lohengrin*.

BIBLIOGRAPHY

PRIMARY

Adam of Eynsham, *Magna Vita Sancti Hugonis: The Life of St Hugh of Lincoln*, ed. and tr. Decima L. Douie and David Hugh Farmer, 2 vols (Oxford: Clarendon Press, 1985)

Aelian, *Characteristics of Animals*, ed. and tr. A. F. Scholfield, 3 vols (Cambridge, MA: Harvard University Press, 1959)

Aeschylus, *Agamemnon*, in *Oresteia*, ed. and tr. Hugh Lloyd-Jones (London: William Heinemann, 1971)

Aesop, *The Complete Fables*, tr. Olivia and Robert Temple (London: Penguin, 1998)

Alan of Lille, *The Plaint of Nature*, in *Literary Works*, ed. and tr. Winthrop Wetherbee (Cambridge, MA: Harvard University Press, 2013)

Albert of Aachen, *Historia Ierosolimitana: History of the Journey to Jerusalem*, ed. and tr. Susan B. Edgington (Oxford: Clarendon Press, 2007)

Albertus Magnus, *De Animalibus: XIII–XXVI*, ed. Hermann Stadler, *Beiträge zur Geschichte der Philosophie des Mittelalters* XXVI (Münster: Aschendorffschen, 1920)

— *On Animals: A Medieval Summa Zoologica*, tr. Kenneth F. Kitchell Jr. and Irven Michael Resnick, 2 vols (Columbus: Ohio State University Press, 2018)

Alexander Neckam, *De Naturis Rerum*, ed. Thomas Wright (London: Longman, Green, Longman, Roberts, and Green, 1863)

Aquinas, Thomas, *Summa Theologiae, Volume 29*, ed. and tr. Thomas Gilby (London: Eyre and Spottiswoode, 1969)

Aristotle, *History of Animals: Books VII–X*, ed. and tr. D. M. Balme (Cambridge, MA: Harvard University Press, 1991)

Batholomaeus Anglicus, *On the Properties of Things: John Trevisa's Translation of Bartholomaeus Anglicus De Proprietatibus Rerum*, ed. M. C. Seymour, 3 vols (Oxford: Clarendon Press, 1975)

Bestiary: Being an English Version of the Bodleian Library, Oxford, MS Bodley 764, tr. Richard Barber (Woodbridge: Boydell Press, 1999)

The Book of Beasts: Being a Translation from a Latin Bestiary of the Twelfth Century, tr. T. H. White (London: Jonathan Cape, 1954)

Calendar of Patent Rolls, 1232–1509, Public Records Office, 53 vols (London, 1891–1916)

Carmina Burana, ed. Peter Diemer, Dorothee Diemer, Benedikt Konrad Vollman (Berlin: Deutscher Klassiker Verlag, 2016)

— *Selections from the Carmina Burana*, tr. David Parlett (Middlesex: Penguin, 1986)

Caxton, William, *The Booke of Ovyde Named Methamorphose*, ed. Richard J. Moll (Oxford: The Bodleian Library, 2013)

La Chanson d'Antioche, ed. Suzanne Duparc-Quioc, 2 vols (Paris: Paul Geuthner, 1977)

The Chanson d'Antioche: An Old French Account of the First Crusade, tr. Susan B. Edgington and Carol Sweetenham (Farnham: Ashgate, 2011)

Chaucer, Geoffrey, 'The Summoner's Tale', in *The Riverside Chaucer*, ed. Larry D. Benson (Oxford: Oxford University Press, 1987), pp. 129–36

Chevelere Assigne, in *Medieval English Romances*, ed. Diane Speed, 2 vols (Durham: Durham Medieval Texts, 1993), pp. 149–70

Le Chevalier au Cygne and La Fin d'Elias, ed. Jan A. Nelson, *The Old French Crusade Cycle*: *Volume* II (Tuscaloosa: University of Alabama Press, 1985)

Cicero, *De Oratore*, in *On the Orator*, ed. and tr. H. Rackham (Harvard: Harvard University Press, 1942)

Close Rolls of the Reign of Henry III: 1247–51, Public Record Office (London: H. M. Stationery Office, 1922)

La Conquête de Jérusalem, ed. Célestin Hippeau (Paris: A. Aubry, 1868)

The Continuations of the Old French 'Perceval' of Chrétien de Troyes, ed. William Roach, 5 vols (Philadelphia: American Philosophical Society, 1952)

Copland, Robert, *The History of Helyas, Knight of the Swan* (London: William Pickering, 1827)

Crane, Walter, *An Artist's Reminiscences* (London: Methuen, 1907)

Curye on Inglysch: English Culinary Manuscripts of the Fourteenth Century, ed. Constance B. Hieatt and Sharon Butler (Oxford: Oxford University Press, 1985)

Durham Priory Manorial Accounts, 1277–1310, ed. Richard Britnell (Woodbridge: Boydell Press, 2014)

Elliot, Daniel Giraud, *The Wild Fowl of the United States and British Possessions* (London: Suckling, 1898)

Les Enfances Godefroi and Le Retour de Cornumarant, ed. Emanuel J. Mickel, *The Old French Crusade Cycle*: *Volume* III (Tuscaloosa: University of Alabama Press, 1999)

Eratosthenes and Hyginus, *Constellation Myths with Aratus's Phaenomena*, tr. Robin Hard (Oxford: Oxford University Press, 2015)

The Exeter Book, ed. George Philip Krapp and Elliott van Kirk Dobbie, *Anglo-Saxon Poetic Records*, vol. 3 (London: George Routledge, 1936)

Extracts from the Municipal Records of the City of York during the Reigns of Edward IV, Edward V, and Richard II, ed. Robert Davies (London: J. B. Nichols and Son, 1843)

Friedrich von Schwaben aus der Stuttgarter Handschrift, ed. Max Hermann Jellinek (Berlin: Weidmannsche, 1904)

Fulgentius, *Mythographi* in *Auctores Mythographi Latini*, ed. Augustino van Staveren (Lugduni Batavorum: Samuelem Luchtmans, J. Wetstenium, and G. Smith, 1742)

— *Mythologies*, tr. Leslie George Whitbread (Columbus: Ohio State University Press, 1971)

Graelent in *French Arthurian Literature: IV Eleven Old French Narrative Lays*, ed. and tr. Glyn S. Burgess and Leslie C. Brook (Cambridge: D. S. Brewer, 2007)

Gerald of Wales, *The History and Topography of Ireland*, tr. John J. O'Meara (London: Penguin, 1982)

— *The Life of St. Hugh of Avalon, Bishop of Lincoln 1186–1200*, ed. and tr. Richard M. Loomis (New York: Garland Publishing, 1985)

Gower, John, *Poems on Contemporary Events: the* Visio Anglie (1381) *and* Cronica tripertita (1400), ed. David R. Carlson, tr. A. G. Rigg (Toronto: Pontifical Institute of Mediaeval Studies, 2011)

Guingamor, in *French Arthurian Literature: IV Eleven Old French Narrative Lays*, ed. and tr. Glyn S. Burgess and Leslie C. Brook (Cambridge: D. S. Brewer, 2007)

Heraclius, *Sermo Augustino praesente*, in *Patrologia Latina*, ed. by J. P. Migne (Paris: Garnier, 1852), 39:1717

Herbert, *Le Roman de Dolopathos*, ed. Jean-Luc Leclanche, 3 vols (Paris: Honoré Champion, 1997)

Historia Vitae et Regni Ricardi Secundi, ed. George B. Stow (Philadelphia: University of Pennsylvania Press, 1977)

Hugh of Fouilloy, *The Medieval Book of Birds: Hugh of Fouilloy's Aviarium*, ed. and tr. Willene B. Clark (Binghamton, NY: Medieval & Renaissance Texts & Studies, 1992)

Irving, Washington, *Astoria or Anecdotes of an Enterprise beyond the Rocky Mountains* (New York: George P. Putnam, 1849)

Isidore of Seville, *Etymologiarum sive originum libri* XX, ed. W. M. Lindsay, 2 vols (Oxford: Clarendon Press, 1911)

—— *The Etymologies of Isidore of Seville*, tr. Stephen A. Barney, W. J. Lewis, J. A. Beach, and Oliver Berghof (Cambridge: Cambridge University Press, 2006)

Johannis de Alta Silva, *Dolopathos: Sive de Rege et Septem Sapientibus*, ed. Hermann Oesterley (Strassburg: Karl J. Trübner, 1873)

— *Dolopathos*, tr. Brady B. Gilleland (Binghamton: State University of New York, 1981)

Jonson, Ben, 'To the Memory of my Beloved Master William Shakespeare', in *The Poetical Works of William Shakespeare and Ben Jonson* (Boston: Houghton Mifflin, 1880)

Konrad von Würzburg, *Der Schwanritter*, ed. Franz Roth (Frankfurt am Main: C. Naumann, 1861)

Lactantius, *Phoenix*, in *Minor Latin Poets*, ed. and tr. J. Wight Duff and Arnold M. Duff (London: William Heinemann, 1934)

La Naissance du Chevalier au Cygne: Elioxe and Beatrix, ed. Emanuel J. Mickel, Jr. and Jan A. Nelson, *The Old French Crusade Cycle*, vol. 1 (Tuscaloosa: University of Alabama Press, 1977)

Master Chiquart, *De fait de cuisine / On Cookery of Master Chiquart* (1420), ed. and tr. Terence Scully (Tempe: Arizona Center for Medieval and Renaissance Studies, 2010)

Maurus, Rabanus, *De Universo*, in *Patrologia Latina* (Paris: J. P. Migne, 1852) 111:9–258c

— *De Universo*, tr. Priscilla Throop, 2 vols (Charlotte, VT: Medieval MS, 2009)

A Medieval Book of Beasts: The Second-Family Bestiary, ed. and tr. Willene B. Clark (Woodbridge: Boydell Press, 2006)

The Middle English Text of Caxton's Ovid, *Books II–III, with a Parallel Text of The Ovide moralisé en prose* II, ed. Wolfgang Mager (Heidelberg: Universitätsverlag Winter, 2016)

Moschus, 'Lament For Bion', in *Theocritus, Moschus, Bion*, ed. and tr. Neil Hopkinson (Cambridge, MA: Harvard University Press, 2015)

A Noble Boke off Cookry ffor a Prynce Houssolde, ed. Robina Napier (London: Elliot Stock, 1882)

O'Curry, Eugene, 'The Trí thruaighe na scéalaigheachta of Erinn: II The Fate of the Children of Lir', *Atlantis*, 4 (1863), 113–57

Olivier de la Marche, *Mémoires d'Olivier de la Marche*, ed. Henri Beaune and J. d'Arbaumont (Paris: Henri Loones, 1884)

On the Orders, Laws and Ancient Customes of Swanns (London: August Mathewes, 1632)

Order for Swannes, England and Wales (London: Henrie Denham, 1584)

The Order for Swannes both by the Statutes, and by the Auncient Orders and Customes vsed within the Realme of England (London: *c.*1615–20)

Origenes, *Origenes Werke: Homilién zu Samuel I, zum Hohelied und zu den Propheten Kommentar zum Hohelied*, ed. W. A. Baehrens (Leipzig: J. C. Hinrich, 1925)

Orff, Carl, *Carmina Burana: Cantiones profanae* (Mainz: B. Schott's Söhne, 1956)

Ovid, *Fasti*, ed. and tr. James George Frazer (London: William Heinemann, 1931)

— *Metamorphoses*, ed. and tr. Frank Justus Miller, 2 vols (London: William Heinemann, 1968)

— *Metamorphoses*, tr. Anthony S. Kline (Ann Arbor: Borders Classics, 2004)

— *Metamorphoses*, tr. Charles Martin, *Norton Critical Edition* (New York: W. W. Norton, 2010)

Ovide Moralisé: poème du commencement du quatorzième siècle, ed. C. de Boer, 3 vols (Amsterdam: Johannes Müller, 1920)

Physiologus: A Medieval Book of Nature Lore, tr. Michael J. Curley (Chicago: University of Chicago Press, 2009)

Plato, *Phaedo*, in *Euthyphro, Apology, Crito, and Phaedo*, ed. and tr. Harold North Fowler (Cambridge, MA: Harvard University Press, 1914)

Pliny, *Natural History, Volume III: Books 8–11*, ed. and tr. H. Rackham (London: William Heinemann, 1940)

Political Poems and Songs Relating to English History, ed. Thomas Wright, vol. 1 (London: Longman, Green, Longman, & Roberts, 1859)

The Quest of the Holy Grail, tr. P. M. Matarasso (Middlesex: Penguin, 1969)

La Queste del Saint Graal, ed. Albert Pauphilet (Paris: Édouard Champion, 1923)

The Red Book of the Exchequer: Volume 2, ed. Hubert Hall (Cambridge: Cambridge University Press, 2012)

Rous, John, *The Rous Roll*, ed. Charles Ross (Gloucester: Alan Sutton, 1980)

Thomas of Cantimpré, *Liber de Natura Rerum*, ed. Helmut Boese, 2 vols (Berlin: Walter de Gruyter, 1973)

Tolkien, J. R. R., *The Return of the King* (New York: Ballantine Books, 1965)

The Tretyse of Loue, ed. John H. Fisher (London: Oxford University Press, 1951)

Vincent of Beauvais, *Speculum Naturale* (Venice: Hermannus Liechtenstein, 1494)

Virgil, *Aeneid: VII–XII*, ed. and tr. H. Rushton Fairclough, 2 vols (London: William Heinemann, 1986)

The Vivendier: A Fifteenth-Century French Cookery Manuscript, ed. and tr. Terence Scully (Totnes: Prospect Books, 1997)

Völundarkviða, in *The Poetic Edda: Volume II Mythological Poems*, ed. and tr. Ursula Dronke (Oxford: Clarendon Press, 1997)

William of Tyre, *A History of Deeds Done Beyond the Sea*, tr. Emily Atwater Babock and A. C. Krey, 2 vols (New York: Columbia University Press, 1943)

— *Chronicon*, ed. R. B. C. Huygens (Turnholt: Brepols, 1986)

Wolfram von Eschenbach, *Parzival*, ed. Joachim Bumke (Tübingen: Max Niemeyer, 2008)

— *Parzival*, tr. A. T. Hatto (London: Penguin, 1980)

SECONDARY

Ahl, Frederick M., 'Amber, Avallon, and Apollo's Singing Swan', *The American Journal of Philology*, 103/4 (1982), 373–411

Arnott, W. Geoffrey, 'Swan Songs', *Greece & Rome*, 24/2 (1977), 149–53

Backhouse, Janet, *Medieval Birds in the Sherborne Missal* (London: British Library, 2001)

Barron, W. R. J., '*Chevalere Assigne* and the *Naissance du Chevalier au Cygne*', *Medium Ævum*, 36/1 (1967), 25–37

— 'Versions and Texts of the *Naissance du Chevalier au Cygne*', *Romania*, 89 (1968), 481–538

Bennett, Michael, 'Gower, Richard II, and Henry IV', in Stephen H. Rigby and Siân Echard (eds), *Historians on John Gower* (Cambridge: D. S. Brewer, 2019), pp. 209–42

Birkhead, Mike, and Christopher Perrins, *The Mute Swan* (London: Croom Helm, 1986)

Bitterli, Dieter, *Say What I Am Called: The Old English Riddles of the Exeter Book and the Anglo-Latin Riddle Tradition* (Toronto: University of Toronto Press, 2009)

Brears, Peter, *Cooking and Dining in Medieval England* (Totnes: Prospect Books, 2008)

Bonsack, Edwin, Dvalinn: *The Relationship of the Friedrich Von Schwaben, Vǫlundarkviða, and Sǫrla Þáttr* (Wiesbaden: Franz Steiner Verlag, 1983)

Boulton, D'Arcy Jonathan Dacre, *The Knights of the Crown: The Monar-chical Orders of Knighthood in Later Medieval Europe, 1325–1520* (Woodbridge: Boydell Press, 2000)

Bullock-Davies, Constance, *Menestrellorum Multitudo: Minstrels at a Royal Feast* (Cardiff: University of Wales Press, 1978)

Busby, Keith, 'The Continuations', in Glyn S. Burgess and Karen Pratt (eds), *The Arthur of the French: The Arthurian Legend in Medieval French and Occitan Literature* (Cardiff: University of Wales Press, 2006), pp. 222–47

Cabot, David, *Wildfowl* (London: Collins, 2009)

Calmette, Joseph, *The Golden Age of Burgundy: The Magnificent Dukes and their Courts*, tr. Doreen Weightman (London: Weidenfeld and Nicolson, 1962)

Martha Carlin, 'Gower's Life', in Stephen H. Rigby and Siân Echard (eds), *Historians on John Gower* (Cambridge: D. S. Brewer, 2019), pp. 32–85

Cazelles, Raymond, and Johannes Rathofer, *Illuminations of Heaven and Earth: The Glories of the Très Riches Heures du Duc de Berry* (New York: Harry N. Abrams, 1988)

Cherry, John, 'The Dunstable Swan Jewel', *Journal of the British Archaeological Association*, 32/1 (1969), 38–53

Clark, James, G., Frank T. Coulson, Kathryn L. McKinley (eds), *Ovid in the Middle Ages* (Cambridge: Cambridge University Press, 2011)

Cramp, Stanley, et al. (eds), *Handbook of the Birds of Europe, the Middle East, and North Africa: The Birds of the Western Palearctic, Volume 1: Ostrich to Ducks* (Oxford: Oxford University Press, 1977)

Crane, Susan, *The Performance of Self: Ritual, Clothing, and Identity During the Hundred Years War* (Philadelphia: University of Pennsylvania Press, 2002)

Crombie, A. C., *Augustine to Galileo: Vol. I, Science in the Middle Ages, V–XIII Centuries* (London: William Heinemann, 1957)

Cross, Tom Peete, 'The Celtic Elements in the Lays of *Lanval* and *Graelent'*, *Modern Philology*, 12/10 (1915), 585–644

D'Avray, D. L., *The Preaching of the Friars: Sermons Diffused from Paris before* 1300 (Oxford: Clarendon Press, 1985)

Davenport, Tony, 'Abbreviation and the Education of the Hero in *Chevalere Assigne'*, in Phillipa Hardman (ed.), *The Matter of Identity in Medieval Romance* (Cambridge: D. S. Brewer, 2002), pp. 9–20

Delacour, Jean, *The Waterfowl of the World*, vol. 4 (London: Country Life Limited, 1964)

Delany, Simon, Jeremy J. D. Greenwood, and Jeff Kirby, 'National Mute Swan Survey 1990', *Report to the Joint Nature Conservation Committee* (February, 1992)

D'Hulst, Roger A., *Flemish Tapestries from the Fifteenth to the Eighteenth Century* (Brussels: Editions Arcade, 1967)

Fox-Davies, Arthur Charles, *A Complete Guide to Heraldry* (London: Thomas Nelson and Sons, 1950)

Desing, Julius, *The Royal Castle of Neuschwanstein*, tr. Bonny Schmid-Burleson (Lechbruck: Wilhelm Kienberger, 1998)

Viscount Dillon, and W. H. St John Hope, 'Inventory of the Goods and Chattels Belonging to Thomas, Duke of Gloucester', *Archaeological Journal*, 54/1 (1897), 275–308

Dronke, Peter, 'The Beginnings of the Sequence', *Beiträg zur Geschichte der deutschen Sprache und Literatur*, 87 (1965), 43–73

Duffin, Ross W. (ed), *A Performer's Guide to Medieval Music* (Bloomington: Indiana University Press, 2000)

Eger, Manfred, 'The Patronage of King Ludwig II', tr. John Deathridge, in Ulrich Müller, Peter Wapnewski (eds), *Wagner Handbook* (Cambridge, MA: Harvard University Press, 1992), pp. 317–26

Gastaldelli, Ferruccio, 'Una Sconosciuta Redazione Latina della *Chanson du Chevalier au Cygne* nel *Commento All'Apocalisse* di Goffredo d'Auxerre', *Aevum*, 42 (1968), pp. 491–501

George, Wilma, and Brunsdon Yapp, *The Naming of the Beasts* (London: Duckworth, 1991)

Given-Wilson, Chris, 'Richard II and the Higher Nobility', in Anthony Goodman and James Gillespie (eds), *Richard II: The Art of Kingship* (Oxford: Clarendon Press, 1999), pp. 107–28

— *The Royal Household and the King's Affinity: Service, Politics and Finance in England* 1360–1413 (London: Yale University Press, 1986)

Godman, Peter, *Poetry of the Carolingian Renaissance* (London: Duckworth, 1985)

Goodall, John A., 'Heraldry in the Decoration of English Medieval Manuscripts', *The Antiquaries Journal*, 77 (1997), 179–220

Hablot, Laurent, 'Emblèmatique et mythologie médiévale, le cygne, une devise princière', *Histoire de l'art*, 49 (2001), 51–64

Hall, Alaric, *Elves in Anglo-Saxon England* (Woodbridge: Boydell Press, 2007)

Hardie, P. R., 'Aeneas and the Omen of the Swans (Verg. Aen. l. 393–400)', *Classical Philology*, 82/2 (1987), 145–50

Hatto, A. T., 'The Swan Maiden: A Folk-tale of North Eurasian Origin?', *Bulletin of the School of Oriental and African Studies*, 24/2 (1961), 326–52

Hope, W. H. St John, 'The Funeral, Monument, and Chantry Chapel of King Henry the Fifth', *Archaeologia*, 65 (1914), 128–86

Jackson, W. H., 'Lorengel and the Spruch von den Tafelrundern', in W. H. Jackson and S. A. Ranawake (eds), *The Arthur of the Germans: The Arthurian Legend in Medieval German and Dutch Literature* (Cardiff: University of Wales Press, 2000), pp. 181–3

Jaffray, Robert, *The Two Knights of the Swan, Lohengrin and Helyas* (New York: G. P. Putnam's Sons, 1910)

John, Simon, 'Godfrey of Bouillon and the Swan Knight', in Simon John and Nicholas Morton (eds), *Crusading and Warfare in the Middle Ages* (London: Routledge, 2014), pp. 129–42

— '"Li bons dus de buillon": Genre Conventions and the Depiction of Godfrey of Bouillon in the *Chanson d'Antioche* and the *Chanson de Jérusalem*', in Andrew D. Buck and Thomas W. Smith (eds), *Remembering the Crusades in Medieval Texts and Songs* (Cardiff: University of Wales Press, 2019), pp. 83–100

Johnsgard, Paul A., *Handbook of Waterfowl Behavior* (London: Constable & Co., 1965)

— *Swans: Their Biology and Natural History* (Lincoln: University of Nebraska Press, 2016)

Jolly, Karen, Catharina Raudvere, Edward Peters, *Witchcraft and Magic in Europe: The Middle Ages* (London: Athlone Press, 2002)

Juethe, Erich, *Der Minnesänger Hiltbolt von Schwangau* (Hildesheim: Georg Olms Verlag, 1977)

Katzenstein, Ranee, and Emilie Savage-Smith, *The Leiden Aratea: Ancient Constellations in a Medieval Manuscript* (Malibu: J. Paul Getty Museum, 1988)

Kear, Janet (ed.), *Ducks, Geese and Swans*, vol. 1 (Oxford: Oxford University Press, 2005)

Keen, Maurice, *Chivalry* (New Haven: Yale University Press, 1984)

Klingender, Francis, *Animals in Art and Thought to the End of the Middle Ages* (London: Routledge & Kegan Paul, 1971)

Leaf, Helen, 'English Medieval Bone Flutes: A Brief Introduction', *The Galpin Society Journal*, 59 (2006), 13–19

Lecouteux, Claude, 'Zur Entstehung der Schwanrittersage', *Zeitschrift für deutsches Altertum und deutsche Literatur*, 107 (1978), 18–33

Lewis, C. S., *The Discarded Image: An Introduction to Medieval and Renaissance Literature* (Cambridge: Cambridge University Press, 1964)

Liver, Ricarda, 'Der singende Schwan: Motivgeschichtliches zu einer Sequenz des 9. Jahrhunderts', *Museum Helveticum*, 39/1 (1982), 146–56

Loomis, Laura Hibbard, *Mediæval Romance in England* (New York: Burt Franklin, 1969)

MacGregor, Arthur, 'Swan Rolls and Beak Markings: Husbandry, Exploitation and Regulation of *Cygnus olor* in England, *c.* 1100–1900', *Anthropozoologica*, 22 (1996), 39–68

March, Jennifer R., *Dictionary of Classical Mythology* (Oxford: Oxbow Books, 2014)

Marks, Richard, and Paul Williamson (eds), *Gothic Art for England 1400–1547* (London: V&A Publications, 2003)

Matthews, Alastair, *The Medieval German Lohengrin: Narrative Poetics in the Story of the Swan Knight* (Rochester, NY: Camden House, 2016)

— 'When is the Swan Knight Not the Swan Knight? Berthold von Holle's *Demantin* and Literary Space in Medieval Europe', *Modern Language Review*, 112/3 (2017), 666–85

McCracken, Peggy, *In the Skin of Beast: Sovereignty and Animality in Medieval France* (Chicago: University of Chicago Press, 2017)

McCulloch, Florence, 'The Dying Swan – A Misunderstanding', *Modern Language Notes*, 74/4 (1959), 289–92

— *Medieval Latin and French Bestiaries* (Chapel Hill: University of North Carolina Press, 1962)

McKendrick, Scot, 'Tapestries from the Low Countries in England during the Fifteenth Century,' in Caroline Barron and Nigel Saul (eds), *England and the Low Countries in the Late Middles Ages* (New York: St Martin's Press, 1995), pp. 43–60

McKinnell, John, 'The Context of *Völundarkviða*', *Saga-Book*, 23 (1990), 1–27

McFarland, Timothy, 'The Emergence of the German Grail Romance', in W. H. Jackson and S. A. Ranawake (eds), *The Arthur of the Germans: The Arthurian Legend in Medieval German and Dutch Literature* (Cardiff: University of Wales Press, 2000), pp. 54–68

Medlicott, R. W., 'Leda and the Swan – An Analysis of the Theme in Myth and Art', *Australian and New Zealand Journal of Psychiatry*, 4 (1970), 15–23

Mills, Robert, 'Jesus as Monster', in Bettina Bildhauer and Robert Mills (eds), *The Monstrous Middle Ages* (Cardiff: Wales University Press, 2003)

Millington, Barry (ed.), *The Wagner Compendium: A Guide to Wagner's Life and Music* (London: Thames and Hudson, 1992)

Morrison, Elizabeth, *Book of Beasts: The Bestiary in the Medieval World* (Los Angeles: The J. Paul Getty Museum, 2019)

Muessig, Carolyn, 'The Sermones Friales et Communes of Jacques de Vitry . . . Part I', *Medieval Sermon Studies*, 47/1 (2003), 33–49

Mynott, Jeremy, *Birds in the Ancient World* (Oxford: Oxford University Press, 2018)

Owen, Myrfyn, *Wildfowl of Europe* (London: Macmillan, 1977)

Pascual, Lucia Diaz, 'The Heraldry of the de Bohun Earls', *The Antiquaries Journal*, 100 (2020), 1–24

Pastoureau, Michel, *Les signes et les songes: Études sur la symbolique et la sensibilité médiévales* (Florence: Sismel-Edizioni del Galluzzo, 2013)

Parker, A. J., 'The Birds of Roman Britain', *Oxford Journal of Archaeology*, 7/2 (1988), 197–226

Pfenning, Andreas R., et al., 'Convergent Transcriptional Specializations in the Brains of Humans and Song-learning Birds', *Science*, 346/6215 (12 December 2014), DOI: 10.1126/science.1256846

Planche, J. R., 'On the Badges of the House of Lancaster', *Journal of the British Archaeological Association*, 6/4 (1851), 374–93

Pollard, A. J., *Late Medieval England, 1399–1509* (Harlow: Pearson Education, 2000)

Price, A. Lindsay, *Swans of the World: In Nature, History, Myth & Art* (Tulsa: Council Oak Books, 1994)

Robertson, Kellie, *Nature Speaks: Medieval Literature and Aristotelian Philosophy* (Philadelphia: University of Pennsylvania Press, 2017)

Rowland, Beryl, *Birds with Human Souls: A Guide to Bird Symbolism* (Knoxville: University of Tennessee Press, 1978)

Saunders, Corinne, *Magic and the Supernatural in Medieval English Romance* (Cambridge: Boydell and Brewer, 2010)

Schofield, William Henry, 'The Lays of Graelent and Lanval, and the Story of Wayland', *PMLA*, 15/2 (1900), 121–80

Scully, Terence, *The Art of Cookery in the Middle Ages* (Woodbridge: Boydell Press, 1995)

Seebohm, Henry, *A History of British Birds: Volume Three* (London: R. H. Porter, 1885)

Siddons, Michael Powell, *Heraldic Badges in England and Wales: Volume II, Part 1, Royal Badges* (Woodbridge: Boydell Press, 2009)

Silvia, Daniel S., Jr., 'Chaucer's Friars: Swans or Swains? *Summoner's Tale*, D 1930', *English Language Notes*, 1 (1964), 248–50

Sloane, Thomas, 'Crane, Walter', in *The Arthurian Encyclopedia*, ed. Norris Lacy (Woodbridge: Boydell Press, 1986), p. 123

Stratford, Jenny, *Richard II and the English Royal Treasure* (Woodbridge: Boydell Press, 2012)

Stevens, John, *Words and Music in the Middle Ages: Song, Narrative, Dance and Drama, 1050–1350* (Cambridge: Cambridge University Press, 1986)

Tait, Hugh, 'Pilgrim-Signs and Thomas, Earl of Lancaster', *British Museum Quarterly*, 20 (1955), 39–47

Taylor, Moss, 'The Polish swan in Britain & Ireland', *British Birds*, 111 (2018), 10–24

Tibbals, Kate Watkins, 'Elements of Magic in the Romance of William of Palerne', *Modern Philology*, 1 (1904), 355–71

Ticehurst, Norman F., *The Mute Swan in England* (London: Cleaver-Hume Press, 1957)

— 'The Mute Swan in Kent', *Archaeologia Cantiana*, 47 (1935), 55–70

Thompson, D'Arcy Wentworth, A *Glossary of Greek Birds* (London: Oxford University Press, 1936)

Thompson, Stith, *The Folktale* (New York: Holt, Rinehart, and Winston, 1946)

Threlfall-Holmes, Miranda, *Monks and Markets: Durham Cathedral Priory* 1460–1520 (Oxford: Oxford University Press, 2005)

Todd, Henry Alfred, 'La Naissance du Chevalier au Cygne ou les Enfants Changes en Cygnes', *Modern Language Association*, 4 (1889), i–xv

Vale, Juliet, *Edward III and Chivalry: Chivalric Society and Its Context* 1270–1350 (Woodbridge: Boydell Press, 1982)

Vale, Malcolm, *War and Chivalry* (London: Duckworth, 1981)

Van den Abeele, Baudouin, 'Trente et un nouveaux manuscrits de l'*Aviarium*: regards sur la diffusion de l'œuvre d'Hugues de Fouilloy', *Scriptorium*, 57/2 (2003), 253–71

Vaughan, Richard, *Philip the Good: The Apogee of Burgundy* (Woodbridge: Boydell Press, 1970)

Wackett, Jayne, 'The Litlyngton Missal: Its Patron, Iconography, and Messages' (unpublished PhD thesis, University of Kent, 2014)

Wagner, Anthony R., 'The Swan Badge and the Swan Knight', *Archaeologia*, 97 (1959), 127–38

Ward, Matthew, *The Livery Collar in Late Medieval England and Wales* (Woodbridge: Boydell Press, 2016)

Williamson, Craig, *Old English Riddles of the Exeter Book* (Chapel Hill: University of North Carolina Press, 1977)

Wilmore, Sylvia Bruce, *Swans of the World* (New York: Taplinger Publishing Co., 1974)

Witherby, H. F., F. C. R. Jourdain, Norman F. Ticehurst, and Bernard

W. Tucker (eds), *The Handbook of British Birds*, vol. 3 (London: H. F. & G. Witherby, 1840)

Witteveen, Joop, 'On Swans, Cranes, and Herons: Part 1, Swans', *Petits Propos Culinaires*, 24 (1986), 22–31

Yarrell, William, A *History of British Birds*, vol. 4 (London: John van Voorst, 1884–5)

WEBSITES / NEWS ARTICLES

Chetham Library, Swan Markings, Thames, late 16th century, 1/422: *https://library.chethams.com/collections/101-treasures-of-chethams/register-of-swan-marks/*

Dyers' Company: *https://www.dyerscompany.co.uk*

Eleanor de Bohun, Duchess of Gloucester', Westminster Abbey, 13 April 2022: *https://www.westminster-abbey.org/abbey-commemorations/commemorations/eleanor-de-bohun-duchess-of-gloucester*

'Florida Sells City Swans after Queen's Gift Leads to Overpopulation', BBC, 18 October 2020: *https://www.bbc.co.uk/news/world-us-canada-54572788*

Lowe, Christopher, 'The Most Popular Pub Names in 2019', in *The Morning Advertiser*, 22 May 2019, *https://www.morningadvertiser.co.uk/Article/2019/05/22/What-are-the-most-popular-pub-names-in-the-*UK

OED *Online.* March 2021. Oxford University Press. *https://www-oed-com*

Order for Swannes, 1584: *https://quod.lib.umich.edu/e/eebo/*A22842.0001.001/1:1?*rgn=div1;view=fulltext*

Order for Swannes, c.1615–20: *https://quod.lib.umich.edu/e/eebo2/*A22848.0001.001/1:2?*rgn=div1;view=fulltext*

Order for Swannes, 1632: *https://quod.lib.umich.edu/e/eebo2/A15665.*0001.001?*view=toc*

Parker, Sam, 'Police Force Gallery to Remove Leda and the Swan Image for 'Condoning Bestiality', *Huffington Post* UK, 30 April

2012: *https://www.huffingtonpost.co.uk/2012/04/30/gallery-swan-image-condones-bestiality_n_1463675.html*

Royal swans: *http://www.royalswan.co.uk/* and *http://www.royalswan.co.uk/pdf/*Royal-Swan-Upping-Brochure.pdf

Schloss Neuschwanstein, Bayerische Schlösserverwaltung, *https://www.neuschwanstein.de/englisch/idea/schwan.htm* (accessed 22 January 2022)

Vintners' Company: *https://www.vintnershall.co.uk*

ONLINE SOURCES FOR IMAGES

Figure 1. Bestiary image of swan, *http://www.bl.uk/manuscripts/Viewer.aspx?ref=harley_ms_4751_f041v*

Figure 2. Swan as constellation, *https://digitalcollections.nypl.org/items/510d47da-eb7e-a3d9-e040-e00a18064a99*

Figure 3. *Clingam, filii, https://gallica.bnf.fr/ark:/12148/btv1b8432316d/f573.item*

Figure 4. Knight of the Swan, *https://digital.bodleian.ox.ac.uk/objects/ccc9f02f-96a8-4bbd-8cf4-5feaa1ae43a5/surfaces/8f74943c-e6c2-4f71-a13e-7eca0f91a159/*

Figure 5. Lohengrin in armour with swan in boat, *https://digi.ub.uni-heidelberg.de/diglit/cpg345/0052*

Figure 6. Lohengrin departs in boat pulled by swan, *https://digi.ub.uni-heidelberg.de/diglit/cpg345/0361*

Figure 7. Swan pilgrim badge, *https://www.britishmuseum.org/collection/object/H_1871-0714-72*

Figure 8. The Nine Worthies: © Raimond Spekking / CC BY-SA 4.0, *https://commons.wikimedia.org/wiki/File:9_gute_Helden_im_Hansasaal_des_Rathauses_Köln_-_Gesamtansicht,_crop-6243.jpg*

Figure 10. Seal of Humphrey de Bohun, *https://scalar.missouri.edu/vm/vol1plates28-33-barons-letter-of-1301*

Figure 11. Margaret de Bohun's tomb, *https://commons.wikimedia.org/wiki/File:BohunSwansCourtenayEffigiesExeterCathedral.jpg*

Figure 12. Bohun Swan in Sherborne Missal, *http://access.bl.uk/item/viewer/ark:/81055/vdc_100104060212.0x000001*, p. 365

Figure 13. Flag of Buckinghamshire, https://www.flaginstitute.org/wp/flags/buckinghamshire-flag/

Figure 14. Arms of Henry IV in Sherborne Missal, *http://access.bl.uk/item/viewer/ark:/81055/vdc_100104060212.0x000001*, p. 80

Figure 15. Arms of Henry, Prince of Wales in Sherborne Missal, *http://access.bl.uk/item/viewer/ark:/81055/vdc_100104060212.0x000001*, p. 81

Figure 16. Ticehurst's English Swan Markings, *https://www.kentarchaeology.org.uk/Research/Pub/ArchCant/Vol.047%20-%201935/047-03.pdf*

Figure 17. British Library Swan Marks, *https://www.bl.uk/catalogues/illuminatedmanuscripts/ILLUMIN.ASP?Size=mid&IllID=28208*

Figure 18. Neuschwanstein, *https://www.loc.gov/pictures/item/2002696255/*

Plate 1. Swans Sing to Human Lyre, *https://digital.bodleian.ox.ac.uk/objects/dd9d1160-196b-48a3-9427-78c209689c1f/surfaces/6de12fc4-03f7-4ac8-b679-9ac0bd5f4ee4/*

Plate 2. Shrewsbury Knight of the Swan and Beatrix giving birth to septuplets, *http://www.bl.uk/manuscripts/Viewer.aspx?ref=royal_ms_15_e_vi_f273r*

Plate 3. Swan Knight Tapestry, Wawel Royal Castle, *https://wawel.krakow.pl/en/textiles*

Plate 4. Saint Hugh of Lincoln, *https://www.artic.edu/artworks/16321/altarpiece-from-thuison-les-abbeville-saint-hugh-of-lincoln*

Plate 5. Chronicle of the Princes of Clèves, *https://gallica.bnf.fr/ark:/12148/btv1b53023935r/f15.item*

Plate 6. Hiltbolt von Schwangao, *https://digi.ub.uni-heidelberg.de/diglit/cpg848/0287*

Plate 7. Arms of Peter de Courtenay, *https://en.wikipedia.org/wiki/ File:BishopPeterCourtenayChimneypieceExeterDetail2.JPG*

Plate 8. Huntington Library Shield with Arms, *https://cdm16003.con- tentdm.oclc.org/digital/collection/p15150coll7/id/49000*

Plate 9. Dunstable Jewel, *https://www.britishmuseum.org/collection/ object/*H_1966-0703-1

Plate 10. Wilton Diptych White Hart, *https://www.nationalgallery.org. uk/paintings/english-or-french-the-wilton-diptych?reverse=*1

OBJECTS

Leda and the Swan, 50–100 BC, marble bust, Roman; London, British Museum, Item No. 1973,0302.1: *https://www.britishmu- seum.org/collection/object/*G_1973–0302–1

La Naissance Scenes on Casket, fifteenth century, bone carving, Italian; London, British Museum, 1885,0804.13: *https://www.brit- ishmuseum.org/collection/object/*H_1885–0804–13. Scenes show- case Matabryne taking seven children, abandoning them in the forest, their rescue by a hermit, a hind providing their nourishment, and the hermit receiving a message from God.

Swan and Otter Hunt, in Devonshire Hunting Tapestries, fifteenth century, textile, the Netherlands; London, V&A Museum, Acces- sion Number T.203-1957: *http://collections.vam.ac.uk/item/*O73327/ *the-devonshire-hunting-tapestries-swan-tapestry-unknown/the- devonshire-hunting-tap*. This image shows grey cygnets, juvenile grey and white swans, and two adult Mute Swans. Unlike the otters, the swans appear to have the upper hand.

INDEX